MW00723745

"With the insight and p
makes some of the least
alive. His compelling and inspiring directives, along with
the key points of application, will motivate you toward
worship, obedience and a keen awareness of how deeply
your heavenly Father loves you. We sometimes forget the
hidden yet powerful truths of these brief books in the
middle of our Bibles. That's about to change! William has
been passionate about "majoring on the Minors" for over
a decade...and I believe his passion for God, God's desires, and God's people reflected in the practical words of
a pastor will impact your life!"

Jeff Young, Minister of Spiritual Development
Prestonwood Baptist Church, Plano, Texas

"It does not require much experience in local church ministry to realize that many believers live in approximately a
third of their Bibles; most of that in the New Testament.
Having engaged in countless conversations with the author about this very topic, I am thrilled that his mind for
biblical truth and his passion for the prophets are now
available for other leaders as well. I cannot recommend
this book highly enough for its breadth of insight and
poignancy, as it speaks as clearly to ministry today as did
the prophets in theirs. Read with pen in hand and take
copious notes. It will be a tool for years to come."

Mike Watson, Pastor of Adult Discipleship
First Baptist Church Concord, Knoxville, Tennessee

"Having worked in leadership positions in churches for over 20 years, both part time and full time, I wish I had read this book earlier in my career. In this book, William Attaway has managed to find and point out valuable leadership lessons from some of those clean white pages in the Bible that we rarely touch. I have never looked at the Minor Prophets from this perspective. I know the points William has made will be beneficial to me as a leader and in my own personal walk with Christ. My only disappointment with this text was when it ended and I realized I had been reading volume 1. Now I'm looking forward to volume 2."

Shawn Stinson, Minister of Music & Outreach
Northside Baptist Church, Jasper, Alabama

Lead.

Leadership Lessons from the (Not So) Minor Prophets

Volume I

William C. Attaway

ERIALL PRESS
Lead. Leadership Lessons from the (Not So) Minor Prophets
William C. Attaway

Published in the United States by Eriall Press

ISBN-13: 978-0615959139
ISBN-10: 061595913-X

DEDICATION

Dedicated with love to my wife and best friend, Charlotte

CONTENTS

ACKNOWLEDGMENTS

There is simply no possible way to acknowledge all of those who have poured into my life and my philosophy of leadership. From teachers to mentors, from professors to pastors, this book is my humble effort to share and add to, in a small way, what has been entrusted to me. I have benefited from learning from leaders as varied as Bill Hybels, Jim Collins, Tommy Briscoe, Patrick Lencioni, Nancy Beach, Jack Welch, Beth Moore, Steven Collins, John Ortberg, Andy Stanley and Dee Whitten, just to name a few. My prayer is that this work reflects the best of these leaders who have poured into me, most from a distance.

This book was written on a sabbatical given to me by the people of Southview Community Church, and I am incredibly grateful for the privilege of having served them as their pastor for nearly ten years now. Thank you for this time to "recharge" and prepare for the next decade of leading and serving with you. Every year I learn more and more what it means to be the people of God as we do life together; thanks for all that you have taught and continue to teach me.

To the staff team I serve with: you are more of a blessing to me and to our church than you know. You continue to challenge me, inspire me, and teach me as we do life and lead together, and I thank God for each of you. The best is yet to come – it's going to be great!

I want to acknowledge the sacrifice of those closest to me: my wife Charlotte and my two daughters, Erin and Allison. They gave up weeks of our being together during my sabbatical so that I could write, and my prayer is that their sacrifice is honored by the results. Your love and encouragement propel me far beyond where I could otherwise go; thank you for showing me in new ways every day what God's love looks like.

And I want to say a special word of thanks to Pat McCormack, who along with Charlotte spent hours proofing the manuscript for this book. Your efforts have made this far better and more readable, and I am very grateful!

Above all, I acknowledge with gratitude my Savior and Lord, Jesus, without Whom none of this would be. I pray that this book brings You glory and honor above all else.

To the glory of God alone,

--William

1 INTRODUCTION

I can remember the first time I heard them speak. Really speak. I was sitting in a classroom in seminary, listening as a professor named Tommy Briscoe spoke about the world the prophets lived in. I began to understand in a fresh way that these men lived in a real time and a real place. Their words were not spoken or written in a vacuum, but in a time and place as real as my own.

Sure, I would have said that was true if you had asked me then, but the separation of culture, time, geography, and language made them "seem" less real than the people I knew. But as I began to understand more about the culture, time, geography, and language of the prophets, I began to understand them not just as the writers of the words on the pages of Scripture, but also as men, as leaders. Some were husbands and fathers; some we don't know about. All lived in difficult and trying times where they didn't always agree with the decisions made by those in charge and where God all too often was relegated to times and places of worship but was not consulted or seen in every day life.

I believe that these twelve men, known infamously as the "Minor Prophets," have much to teach us today if we will but listen.

I've been in vocational ministry now for 17 years, and it has saddened me greatly that these prophets are largely ignored in our day. Rarely are they preached on in our worship services (when's the last time you heard a message on Obadiah?); rarely are they taught on in our Bible classes or small groups; and even more rarely are they used in teaching leadership. The distance between our culture and theirs is not a small one, and the gap in culture, time, geography, and language is quite intimidating to many, causing them to shy away from exploring these books and all that is within them. My goal is to help by mining their depths and assisting with understanding how to bridge these gaps. I believe we can learn a lot from these guys. That's what this book is about.

As a student of leadership for nearly 25 years, I've read voraciously on the subject, I've made appointments and talked with leaders, and I've taken copious notes at more leadership conferences and events than I can count. I've even hosted leadership small groups and gatherings myself, attempting to share what I have learned and raise up new leaders in our local church context. In all of that, I know there is so much I have yet to learn. I am a leadership rookie for sure, but I am committed to being a continual student of this subject for the rest of my life. I'm passionate about leadership, and I'm passionate about helping other people understand what the Bible teaches. My goal when I teach is for the characters and events of the Bible to come alive in the minds of the hearers, and now I wish the same for my readers. This book is my humble effort to try to capture some of the principles that I see in the words of the "Minor Prophets," specifically related to the topic of leadership, and combine these two passions in my own life for the benefit of those who read it.

My hope and prayer is that this book will be helpful and beneficial for you. And know that while I am indebted to all those who have poured into me and my leadership for the last two decades (both in person and from a distance), any mistakes or errors in this book are mine alone. Now, let's jump in and begin to learn together from these (not so) "Minor Prophets."

2 THE "MINOR" PROPHETS

Let's start with a bit of an overview of the prophets we're talking about. In the Bible, there are twelve known as the "Minor Prophets" – Hosea, Joel, Amos, Obadiah, Jonah, Micah, Nahum, Habakkuk, Zephaniah, Haggai, Zechariah, and Malachi. In the Hebrew Bible, they are collectively known as the book of the Twelve. These are all short books compared to what are known as the Major Prophets (Isaiah, Jeremiah, Ezekiel, and Daniel), and their shorter length is why they have been called "minor." However, we have to be careful not to confuse length with value or impact, because these twelve books have both in a major way.

The Minor Prophets' place in history spans from approximately 800 B.C.E. to 450 B.C.E. – that's a significant period of time. If you're familiar with Old Testament biblical history, you'll recall that the golden era for Israel was the time of the United Monarchy, during the reigns of David and Solomon (ca. 1000-922 B.C.E.). After Solomon died in 922 B.C.E., there was a split in the kingdom of Israel. The northern nation (made up of ten of the twelve tribes of Israel) would be known as Israel. The southern nation (made up of the tribes of Judah and Benjamin) would be known as Judah. The northern nation of Israel would exist until 722 B.C.E. when it was conquered and destroyed by the Assyrian Empire. Assyria would last as a major world power until 612 B.C.E. when the capital city of Nineveh fell to the Babylonian Empire.

Judah lasted longer than Israel or Assyria, but met her demise in 586 B.C.E., falling to the Babylonians as well. The people of the northern nation of Israel would not come back together again as a separate nation, but the people of Judah did. In 538 B.C.E., the people were allowed by Cyrus, king of the Persians (who had conquered the Babylonians) to return home and worship God as they wished. Many people went back to the land, and ultimately rebuilt the Temple in 515 B.C.E. and the walls of Jerusalem in 445 B.C.E.

Some of the prophets spoke to the northern nation of Israel; some spoke to the southern nation of Judah; one even spoke to those outside the descendants of Abraham. Some spoke before the Babylonian exile, and some spoke after. But they all spoke ultimately to a people who have been called by God to be distinct, to be His people, and they spoke words reminding the people of what God had done in the past.

The prophets were ordinary men and women doing an extraordinary thing: speaking the words of God to His people. They were spokespeople for God, and contrary to what you might have thought, they were not all men. We see women prophets in the Old Testament, including Miriam, the sister of Moses (Exodus 15:20), Huldah (2 Kings 22:14), Deborah (Judges 4:4), and Noadiah (Neh. 6:14). All of the "writing prophets" (who have books of the Bible attributed to them) were men, which is not surprising given the patriarchal society in which they lived.

Prophets arose very early in the history of Israel. Moses is considered to be the first prophet; Deuteronomy 34:9-10 said that no prophet to equal him had appeared in Israel at the time of its writing. Time and time again, the prophets would quote from the five books of Moses, reminding the people of what God had said and what He had promised.

Along with true prophets, though, came the rise of false prophets, who used the prophetic title and mantle for personal prestige or manipulation. False prophets used scare tactics to frighten their hearers into doing what they said. In the Mosaic Law, God gave the people tests to determine if a prophet's words were authentic (Deuteronomy 13:1-5 and Deuteronomy 18:20-22).

From the time of the divided monarchy, we read of a group called "the sons of the prophets," a prophetic order, or guild, where prophets were trained in the ways of God. We see Elisha in II Kings 6:1-7 shepherding a group from this order. It was from "the sons of the prophets" that most scholars believe the canonical writing prophets of Israel came.

The prophets were a distinct group, called by God to speak to the people on His behalf. They were not all the same. When you read the words of Amos, you get a completely different sense of the kind of man he was compared to the sense you get when you read the words of Jonah. We should think of the prophets primarily as covenant enforcers who reminded the people of the words of the covenant with God, and despite the common modern perception of prophets, they were far more concerned with forth-telling (telling it like it is or should be) than foretelling (telling what will happen in the future).

Were they successful? It depends on how you define the term 'success.' Did they do what God asked them to do? Yes. In that they were successful. Did the people always respond to their words and prophetic actions and signs, repenting and turning back to God? Hardly. Most of the prophets did not see the people respond positively to what they had to say. I can imagine that they were mocked and ridiculed for what they had to say and for what they did. There are two exceptions to that among the Minor Prophets, and we'll talk about both of them in this book, but keep in mind that most of the time, the people of Israel and Judah did not take them seriously.

What we have recorded for us in the pages of the Bible are the messages of these men, spoken on behalf of God, to a people who needed to hear from God (though they didn't always acknowledge that). As we begin to look and mine the pages for their insights, I'd encourage you to do your best to understand them in their world. That's the best way to understand their messages and uncover principles that can benefit you and me today.

3 JONAH

**"The word of the Lord came to Jonah son of Amittai:
'Go to the great city of Nineveh and preach against
it, because its wickedness has come up before me.'"**
– Jonah 1:1-2

I'm starting with Jonah, not because he is first in the
Bible's table of contents listing of the Minor Prophets or
first chronologically in history – he is neither – but simply
because he's one of my favorites. The book of Jonah is
well known; in fact, I'd say he's probably the best-known
Minor Prophet. Children have been told the story of
"Jonah and the Whale" for a long time, songs have been

written, cartoons produced, and flannel graphs utilized. But I'd ask that as we begin, try to look at the story of Jonah with fresh eyes. Try to push aside what you've heard and what you remember and come with new eyes and ears to the book of Jonah.

Other than in the book that bears his name, we know of Jonah also from 2 Kings 14, where we see Jonah giving counsel to King Jeroboam II. Jonah advises the king as God's prophet and tells the king to take advantage of a military situation with their northern neighbor. His counsel resulted in the northern border of Israel being extended as far north as it was during the days of David and Solomon, the entire section that God had given to Abraham, Isaac, and Jacob. It was a time of great rejoicing for the people of Israel, and they were quite proud of what they had done in restoring this territory.

Jonah was probably viewed as a national hero. Here was the man who had advised the king in the greatest military victory and success in many years. Jonah was a very patriotic guy, very committed to his country, and he was used by God to lead the nation to a great victory.

If you can think of people you know who are all "God and Country" (and sometimes you wonder if they always put them in that order), that's a good mental picture of Jonah. He loved God, and he loved the northern nation of Israel.

The book begins by describing how God sent a message to Jonah, which was a common enough occurrence for a prophet. However, the message itself was anything BUT common. God told Jonah to go to Nineveh, the capital of Assyria, and preach against it. God knows all about the wickedness of the people of Assyria, and now he's going to send one of His prophets in to preach to the people of Him and His ways, warning them of judgment and destruction if they don't repent.

Jonah was not a fan of this message. So much so, in fact, that the next thing we see is the back of Jonah as he high tails it out of there, heading for Tarshish. We see, in this story that begins so typically, something very atypical – Jonah says no to God. And it's not just a simple no; it's a no accentuated by running in the opposite direction.

Before we go much farther, I want to stop and talk about the first leadership principle I see in Jonah. It's this: **Everybody answers to somebody**. Not that complicated, I know, but I am continually amazed at how often I see this one ignored. Whether it's in church leadership, political leadership, or business leadership, the principle is true: everybody answers to somebody. Jonah, who was a prophet of God, forgot that. Not only did he decline God's instructions, but he also tried to run from God. That becomes a big problem for Jonah. We talk about God's character and attributes using big words sometimes; we say He is omnipotent (all powerful), omniscient (all knowing), omnibenevolent (all good), and omnipresent (existing everywhere at once). That last one is important in this story; where <u>exactly</u> are you going to run from a God who is everywhere? Jonah would likely have been familiar with Psalm 139, which says,

> **"Where can I go from your Spirit? Where can I flee from your presence? If I go up to the heavens, you are there; if I make my bed in the depths, you are there. If I rise on the wings of the dawn, if I settle on the far side of the sea, even**

**there your hand will guide me, your right
hand will hold me fast."**

Jonah forgot that He answers to God and that he is a man under authority, no matter how much he doesn't like his assignment.

Jonah's running, but God's not going to just let him go. Jonah boards a ship headed for Tarshish, and as the ship is sailing along, God sends a storm. It's a big one, and the experienced sailors on board have never seen anything like it. They are throwing things overboard, trying to lighten the load so they can stay afloat. But where's the prophet? He's below deck, sleeping, completely unconcerned. The captain of the ship comes down to wake him, telling him to pray to his God that they might be saved. Jonah's silent – we don't see him saying anything in response. He knows what's happening here, and he is as stubborn as a mule. I can just hear him saying to himself, "I WILL NOT go!" Can't you hear that said like only a two year old (or stubborn adult) can say it?

WHO'S ROCKING THIS BOAT?

The sailors finally run out of options, and they decide to cast lots (like rolling dice) to determine who's the cause of this. They recognize that this storm is not natural – this is God at work, and somebody's the cause. They cast the lots and who comes up the "winner" but Jonah! Now begins a fast paced game of 20 questions; the sailors want to know who Jonah is and what's behind all of this.

Oh man. Now what? Jonah finally speaks – he tells them who he is, and he tells them that he is running from God. Conditions on the sea are getting worse and worse, and the sailors immediately ask what they should do next. Jonah tells them to pick him up and throw him into the sea – that'll calm everything down and they'll be fine. But the men don't want to do that – life matters more to them than that, so they try to row back to land. But the storm just gets worse and worse, and so finally they do what Jonah had told them to do, and they throw him into the sea. When they do, the sea grows calm. The storm is over.

We read chapter one of Jonah, and it's a familiar story to many of us. Notice something with me: Jonah was willing to do whatever it took NOT to do what God had told him to do, up to and including dying. It might sound noble at first read when Jonah told the men to throw him in the sea to save themselves, but I think what's going on in Jonah's mind was this: if I die, I won't have to go to Nineveh.

Yeah.

What's the deal? Why is he so set against doing what God told him to do?

I think it comes down to this. Nineveh was the enemy of the people of Israel. Nineveh was the capital city of Assyria, an empire known throughout the Ancient Near East for its cruelty, and the people of the northern nation of Israel didn't want anything to do with Assyrians. They hated them. Think about sentiments in America during the 1950's and 1960's toward the Soviet Union; that's what we're talking about. It would be like an American prophet being told to go and preach in Moscow's Red

Square in 1960 so that the people could be saved from God's destruction. Jonah was completely fine with the destruction of Nineveh and the whole nation of Assyria! He didn't want to go there and preach to them; they might respond positively, and then God wouldn't destroy them; Jonah didn't want any part of that. So he ran, choosing to do anything rather than what God said, even if it means he has to drown.

This brings me to my second principle for leaders from Jonah. **Racism and hatred have no place in the life of a leader.**

The pagan sailors on the boat valued life more than Jonah did! These men were a sharp contrast to this prophet of God, weren't they? Jonah had allowed racism and hatred to have full control in his life when it came to the Assyrians. He forgot that every life matters to God. And what matters to God is supposed to matter to His people too.

Too often throughout history, especially in the church, racism has reared its ugly head. Hatred of others who don't look like us (or think like us or act like us) has become what the church is sometimes known for – that's just not ok! Leaders must understand that racism and hared have no place in the life of a leader; they directly contradict the mission that we have been given by God to reach out to ALL people with His message of love. Jonah forgot what God had told Abraham in Genesis 12:1-3, where he talked about the nation that He would create starting with Abram:

"I will make you into a great nation, and I will bless you; I will make your name great, and you will be a blessing. I will bless those who bless you, and whoever curses you I will curse; and <u>all peoples on earth will be blessed through you</u>" (emphasis mine).

All people on earth will be blessed through you – because every life matters to God and must to His people as well.

Far too often, we forget that.

Far too often, we treat others not as people who matter, but as less than that. We treat them as boxes to check, as tasks to accomplish, or as means to an end.

Far too often, we forget that every person God created bears His image and that we should treat them that way.

Even if they don't vote the way we do.

Even if they don't make the choices we think they should make.

Even if their lives don't look anything like ours.

Jonah forgot that God loves ALL people. And so do we sometimes. As leaders, we must remember that racism and hatred have no place in our lives.

INSIDE THE FISH

Jonah's story should end with his dying in the water, but it doesn't. God's not going to let him get away like that. The first chapter of Jonah ends with this: **"Now the Lord provided a huge fish to swallow Jonah, and**

Jonah was in the belly of the fish three days and three nights."

Can you imagine what Jonah had to be thinking? Something like "you have GOT to be kidding me! Seriously God?? Swallowed by and then living inside a big fish?? For 3 DAYS?" Think about the smell alone...

Jonah's not going to get away from his assignment; God's not done with him yet. And sitting in that fish, for three days and nights, Jonah finally understands that. He finally understands that God's not going to let him run away from this. He's going to have to do it.

Have you ever been in a place where you knew what you should do, but you just didn't want to do it? I think we all have. And there comes a point when we realize that we just have to step up and do it even though we'd rather be 1000 miles away doing just about anything else. Tarshish was the end of the known world at the time of Jonah. He'd rather have run to the end of the world than go to Nineveh.

Let me ask you a question. What's your Nineveh?

Leaders, so often we know what needs to be done. We know the next right thing to do, but for whatever reason, we would rather run to the end of the world than do it. Why is that? I think it's because we avoid conflict with every fiber of our being.

That volunteer is not working out in that position – but we'd rather spend an hour surfing Facebook or doing something far less important than have that conversation.

That employee is not working out – but we put off the conversation that needs to be had and justify it by saying, "maybe things will change."

We know that ministry area is not bearing fruit – but we'd rather just focus on what's working right than shut down the unfruitful ministry and make those folks unhappy.

That business decisions looms large in front of us, and we know in our gut what we need to do – but we delay day after day, because we know the repercussions of making the decision could be huge.

I can think of so many times when I've avoided a problem that I knew needed to be dealt with because I didn't want to deal with the mess. And every time I did that, I ended up dealing with it eventually anyway – and it made a much bigger mess than if I'd just acknowledged it and dealt with it at the first.

This mentality is not limited to church leadership. No matter the organization or business, it's very tempting to run the other way from something that we know needs doing. Part of good leadership is running <u>toward</u> the problem, not away from it. And sometimes, it takes a few days in the fish before we are willing to do what we know we need to do.

Jonah gets there, and chapter two is the record of his prayer to God. He focuses on who God is and what He has done, and he ends by saying **"what I have vowed, I will make good."** I will do what you've asked me to do, God.

R. T. Kendall says that "the belly of the fish is not a happy place to live, but is a good place to learn."[1] Jonah begins to learn – he prays to His God, and concludes his prayer with the great statement of faith in this book – **"Salvation comes from the Lord."** Only God can save.

And the chapter ends with God's orchestrating Jonah's release from his "living quarters" inside the great fish. Specifically, the fish spits Jonah out onto dry land. Yeah, that had to be a very memorable experience. Can you imagine? But my favorite part comes in the next verse, the first verse of chapter 3. **"Then the word of the Lord came to Jonah a second time: "Go to the great city of Nineveh and proclaim to it the message I give you."**

Do you know why I like that verse so much? Because it's such a part of who God is – "the word of the Lord came to Jonah a second time." God is a God of second chances, and that's what we see here. God completely starts over and gives Jonah a second chance.

Does he deserve it? Not from what I read in this book so far – but since when do we do anything to deserve God's mercy? God has given me so many second chances, and I imagine the same is true for you. That's who God is – as long as we're breathing, we have another opportunity to come back to Him. As long as we're breathing, we have another chance to do what He asks us to do.

When it comes to giving people around us a second chance, or even giving ourselves one, we tend to think "do they deserve it?" or "do I deserve it?" Is that the right question? What should the question be? Or have we missed the question completely?

THE SHORTEST SERMON EVER

Jonah gets a second chance, and he doesn't let the grass grow under his feet. This time, he goes to Nineveh. He goes into the city and gives what I think is the shortest sermon in the history of the world – **"Forty more days and Nineveh will be overthrown."** Forty more days and God's going to level this place. And that's it. That's the introduction and the body and the closing and the takeaway from his message.

What's the story there? Why so brief?

Though you can argue that he's said all that needs to be said, and you can secretly wish that more preachers followed his example, I think there's something more here that explains the brevity.

Jonah doesn't want them to repent.

Not even one of them.

Remember, Jonah's a very nationalistic guy. These people in Nineveh are the enemy – they are no friends of his or anyone he knows – and the best outcome here from his perspective is that they get completely destroyed, wiped out, nothing left. And he figures that by doing what he does, he checks his box, doing what God told him to do, but not one bit more. He fulfills the letter of the law, but ignores the heart behind it.

It's a textbook picture of legalism. Jonah's checking the boxes while ignoring the heart of God behind them.

THE RESPONSE

So the people of Nineveh finally hear God's message to them through Jonah. What will they do? These are some of the most hardened, cruel, and vicious pagans in the ancient world. What's going to be their response to this single Hebrew prophet who comes and shares a message that is five words long in Hebrew?

The next verse tells us – **"The Ninevites believed God."**

What??

They hear Jonah, they believe what he says, and they act on that belief. From the king to the lowest beggar, a fast is proclaimed, and the king of Nineveh puts on sackcloth and sits down in ashes, a sign of tremendous remorse and grief. And then he issues this proclamation:

"Do not let people or animals, herds or flocks, taste anything; do not let them eat or drink. But let people and animals be covered with sackcloth. Let everyone call urgently on God. Let them give

up their evil ways and their violence. Who knows? God may yet relent and with compassion turn from his fierce anger so that we will not perish."

That's unexpected. The Ninevites took God's message seriously, and they responded with contrite hearts and repentance. And don't think that went unnoticed by God. When He saw their heartfelt response, that they turned away from the violence and evil that they had been doing, He had mercy on them and did not destroy them.

What a great end to this – it doesn't get any better than that, right? Mission accomplished – lives are saved, all's well that ends well.

But we have one more chapter to go.

JONAH'S RESPONSE

What does Jonah think about all this?

"But to Jonah this seemed very wrong, and he became angry."

Seriously Jonah? Your response to a whole city of people's repentance and God's grace and mercy extended is to be angry?

Remember, Jonah wasn't a fan of this mission from day one. And he tells God exactly why.

Jonah is livid. God turns from his anger at the end of chapter 3 and forgives the people of Nineveh when they ask; Jonah is red-faced mad about it. "God, how dare you save those people? They are my enemies, the enemies of my country; this is why I didn't want to come here in the first place!!" As he prays, he quotes Exodus 34 where God gives His name to Moses, throwing God's words back at Him like an angry child – **"gracious and compassionate, slow to anger and abounding in love."**

What a prayer – what words to come from a prophet of God. How real and human is Jonah – how like us sometimes.

Make sure to note the selfishness of Jonah's prayer. The words "I" or "my" occur no fewer than nine times in the Hebrew text here. Nine times in two verses!

Jonah had no problem at all with God's showing love and compassion to him and his country. He just didn't want God to show the same to anyone else or their country. As a preschool teacher might say to two errant kids, "We have a bit of a sharing problem here."

Jonah is praying again for the second time in this book. In chapter two, he prays to God while he is in the belly of the great fish. Here, Jonah prays to God after seeing an entire city saved by God from destruction. Notice the difference in tone – somewhat different, right?

He ends this "prayer" with a request that God kill him; he'd rather die than watch God save the people of Nineveh. He doesn't want to have to watch the mercy of God in action; he'd rather not live. Wow.

In other words, "God, I knew you would do this. I knew you wouldn't destroy them. And I want them

GONE! So just kill me now because I can't stand the sight of these people continuing to exist for one more minute."

Kind of harsh coming from a prophet of God, isn't it?

And yet how often do we have similar feelings about God's grace or blessings being extended to someone else who we think is unworthy? How often are we angry because God doesn't extend a strong dose of what we think is well-deserved justice, but instead offers a hand of love?

If we're honest, Jonah's not alone in his feelings, is he? He's just a lot more honest about it than you and I are sometimes.

Jonah is eaten up with anger and bitterness about what's happened, and his response to all of this is to yell at God. And God replies to Jonah with one sentence:

"Is it right for you to be angry?"

Jonah doesn't answer God's question. We have no indication that Jonah makes out like he hears at all, somewhat like a child.

Jonah moves out east of the city and sits down to wait, watching and hoping that God will change His mind and will indeed destroy the city. He thinks, "Maybe, just maybe, God will do what I want him to do anyway…" From this spot, he'd have a pretty good view of the fireworks if He did destroy it. He is hopeful, but not overly so. It's hot, so he builds a little shelter, kind of like what the people of Israel would build at the Feast of Tabernacles, and he waits.

The destruction Jonah wants doesn't happen. And Jonah continues to pout.

Here's my next principle for leaders from Jonah:

Leaders don't handle the unexpected by pouting.

What does Jonah think his pouting is really going to accomplish? What does he think the next step is going to look like?

He's not thinking. He's just angry. And when we're angry, we handle the unexpected by pouting (or worse). In anger, we can say and do things that we might never do otherwise. And here we get a first hand look at what bitterness and anger can look like: a prophet who is angry that people listened to his message from God and found salvation.

How very sad.

THE VINE

In chapter four, the text tells us that God then provides a vine. That's the same word in Hebrew as when God provided a fish. Who do we see is really in charge here? We know. This vine grows over Jonah's shelter and provides some relief from the sun as it beats down. And Jonah is happy. This is the first time in the whole book that we've seen Jonah happy. This vine makes him giddy; he's ecstatic!

Again in verse 7, God provides. This time, it's a worm that chews the vine so that it withers. Then God provides again – a scorching east wind. This is not nearly as good as the vine! Jonah's not happy anymore. In fact, the text says that he grows faint. He wants to die, and says so again to God. How many times is that now?

God responds to his request by asking him if it's right for him to be angry about the vine. And Jonah fires back at God that it absolutely is right! You can just hear Jonah saying, "Absolutely God – I'm mad as a wet hen, and frankly I wish I were dead." Again.

And God responds once more to Jonah. And you and I need to listen really hard to this.

"But the Lord said, "You have been concerned about this plant, though you did not tend it or make it grow. It sprang up overnight and died overnight. And should I not have concern for the great city of Nineveh, in which there are more than a hundred and twenty thousand people who

cannot tell their right hand from their left—and also many animals?"

"Jonah, you've been concerned about this plant that you didn't create or tend or take care of at all. It grew, lived, and died very quickly. It was of very little value in the grand scheme of things. But Nineveh has more than one hundred and twenty thousand people living there, that I created, who need My compassion. Why do you care more about a plant than about those people? It has a lot of cattle too – do you want them destroyed? Should I not be concerned about that great city?"

What's worth more – a plant or a hundred and twenty thousand people?

God had the first word in the book of Jonah as he spoke to the prophet with the initial call, and here we see that God has the last word. Throughout this book, we see that God is compassionate to all people. We see the initial call to Jonah to go and preach to the people of Nineveh; God is concerned about these folks! We see God's compassion as He saves the men on Jonah's runaway boat;

His love extends to these pagan sailors! We see His mercy extended to the people of Nineveh as they repent and turn to God; He turns from His intent to destroy them because they turn from their wickedness and evil ways.

Ezekiel 33:11 says that God **"takes no pleasure in the death of the wicked, but desires rather that they turn from their ways and live."** 2 Peter 3:9 says that God doesn't want anyone to perish, but for everyone to come to repentance. He is the Father who wants to see every child come home; He is the shepherd who seeks after every lost sheep. Every life matters to God!

Leaders, here's my final principle from Jonah: **People matter more to God than things or tasks (and should to us as well).**

Jonah was more concerned about a plant that gave him some shade for a day than he was about the people of Nineveh. He cared more about a vine with leaves than about humans made in the image of God. God gently corrected him as He taught Jonah about the value of every life. No life is worthless; no life is valueless; no life is disposable. Every life is valuable to God. And every life matters more than things or tasks. It's about people.

Boy, can I think of times I've messed THAT up! I'm a pretty driven, Type A personality. Those around me know I'm all about making lists and crossing things off. Task oriented just barely begins to describe me. And so often, I get a nudge from God to forget the task I'm working on and listen to the person right in front of me because that person matters more than the task does. Would that I always listened! I'm afraid that more often than not, I'm too busy to even listen to that still, small voice. And in talking to other leaders, I find that I'm not alone in this. We have to remember that, as leaders, our work is about people. Sure, the tasks have to get done, and we shouldn't just drop all of our responsibilities to be more relational, but we have to remember that we can be human too! We can listen to those around us. We can pay attention to them. We can invest in those relationships, understanding that the people around us matter to God and should to us as well.

Jonah wanted God to bless his country, and he wanted God to show no mercy to others. His patriotism got in the way of his understanding that God loves all people, regardless of where they live or what they have done. We are all sinners; we all fall short of the glory of God. Not one of us is worth more than another in God's sight. We are all valuable to Him as creations made in His image. Douglas Stuart asks, "What right do we have to demand that God should favor us and not others?"[2] Aren't we all sinners in need of the grace of God?

Philip Cary compares Jonah to other prophets that we know from Scripture. Elijah wanted to die because he saw himself as a failure in his mission as a prophet. Cary says that Jonah is like the anti-Elijah, wanting to die not because his mission seems to have failed, but because it has evidently succeeded. Moses quoted God's name back to Him as he interceded on behalf of the people of God; Jonah is like the anti-Moses, quoting the proclamation of God's name not to intercede, but to complain. Job sought death because his life was harder than he thought he could take; Jonah is like the anti-Job, seeking death not because God is hard, but because He is merciful. Abraham argued back and forth with God trying to save the people of Sodom; Jonah is like the anti-Abraham, arguing with God not in order to save the city that God has threatened to overthrow, but to object to its salvation.[3]

God showed Jonah the fallacy in his thinking in chapter 4. He showed Jonah that grace is extended to all, love is extended to all, and mercy is extended to all. We cannot choose to limit God's grace to others; in fact, as recipients of God's grace, we should be the first to offer grace to others. We live in a world that is in desperate need of the message of God's love and hope, of His forgiveness and mercy. We live in a day when we need hope, and real hope is found only in God.

God is way too merciful for Jonah's taste. Jonah wanted justice (his brand of justice) done; he wanted Nineveh destroyed for her sins and her wickedness. What God showed Jonah (and us) is that he (and we) can't have it both ways. Too often, we want justice for others and grace for ourselves. As sinners, we have no right to insist that God punish another when we have received grace which we do not deserve. When God extends grace and forgiveness to us, we know better than anyone how much we don't deserve it, and we should be the first to offer to others what we have received.

God is so patient with Jonah in this book, and I think with us as well. How many things get in the way of our being the people God wants us to be? How many things do we put before God in our lives? How many things get in the way of our sharing the hope that we have received with people who need it so badly? They can even be good things, like our family, our kids, our career, or our hobbies. Have we allowed even good things to keep us from becoming the people God calls us to be, or to do the greater things that God calls us to do?

God teaches us through the book of Jonah that every life matters to God; every person is made in His image; every life is valuable. When we speak badly of another person, when we say mean and unkind things about others, when we run others down in our conversations – this is not pleasing to our Father. God is not pleased when we treat others who are made in His image as though they are worthless. He wants us to show His love; in fact, that's how we are to be known by the world – by our love for God and for others. Even when we disagree, even when others do things that we don't like, even when we are attacked – Christ followers respond in love. We do that because every life matters in the eyes of our Father.

We want to be like Jesus. We seek to follow Him in every way. Therefore, we must see others as He sees them: as valuable, as made in the image of God. Leaders, we must stop seeing things or tasks as worth more than people; Jesus died for people, for you, for me, for every person who has ever lived or ever will. He did that because of His great love for us. Because Jesus loved us and died for us, we are to love Him and each other.

Robert Chisholm puts it this way: "The Ninevites were no different than Israel or Jonah. All were rebellious sinners deserving only punishment. Yet God had graciously decided to show mercy to both. Jonah was willing to accept this in Israel's case and his own case, but not in Nineveh's."[4] He wanted justice for them and mercy for himself and Israel. Sound familiar at all?

How can we accept God's grace and mercy toward us and refuse to extend it to other people? In light of what we have been forgiven of, in light of what we have been saved from - life separated from God now on this earth and forever in Hell, how can we possible refuse to offer God's love to anyone?

Jonathan Swift is considered by many to be one of the best-known satirists in the English language. During the latter 17th and early 18th centuries, this Irishman penned many works such as *Gulliver's Travels* and *A Modest Proposal*. Swift also wrote poetry, part of one of which expresses what Jonah is communicating I think:

"We are God's chosen few,
all others will be damned.
There is no place in heaven for you,
we can't have heaven crammed."

We are shocked at such sentiment – *we* would *never* vocalize such a statement as this. And yet do we not see Jonah doing just that? It's not apathy he has for the people of Nineveh – it's hatred!

We today are much more enlightened, or so we think. We would never speak such words as Swift penned. I would ask though: do our actions communicate the same message loudly and clearly? By our refusal to treat others as people made in the image of God, by our lack of passion in sharing the hope of the world with people that we know, by our lack of obedience in sharing the hope that we have received with others – do we not in essence communicate those words without saying them?

These four principles from Jonah are far from exhaustive, but perhaps they will get you thinking and seeing yourself more in the life of Jonah than you have before. I think we're more like Jonah sometimes than we'd care to admit. But how wonderful to understand that we know and serve the same God of second chances that we see in the book of Jonah!

PRINCIPLES FROM JONAH:

- Everybody answers to somebody.

- Racism and hatred have no place in the life of a leader.

- Leaders don't handle the unexpected by pouting.

- People matter more to God than things or tasks (and should to us as well).

4 OBADIAH

"The pride of your heart has deceived you..."
--Obadiah 1:3

I remember a few years ago taking a group to the land of Israel for the first time. It was an amazing experience. We saw places that I'd only read about, we saw streets that Jesus would likely have seen in the first century, and we climbed steps that He likely climbed. It was an amazing and exhilarating experience that has added so much to my reading of God's Word. I will never forget it.

On our trip, we saw the place where the Temple once stood, known today as the Temple Mount. We saw some of the walls of the Old City of Jerusalem and the foundation stones for the retaining walls around the Temple complex. The majesty and the presence that is there even among the excavated ruins and the remains of the stones make me marvel at what it must have been like in the first century.

At the Israeli Museum, we saw a detailed model of first century Jerusalem, complete with houses, streets, and, of course, the Temple complex itself. It was absolutely stunning to see what Jerusalem would have looked like then, in the days of Jesus.

It was in Jerusalem that the prophet Obadiah lived in the 6th century before Jesus came to earth. We don't know much about the prophet other than approximately when he lived and ministered. His name means "servant of the Lord," a common name in his day. His is the shortest book in the Old Testament – one chapter, only twenty-one verses long. Yet in this book we find a number of truths and precepts that I believe are beneficial and necessary today.

I heard a favorite Bible teacher of mine, John Ortberg, say in a talk once, "You know, we're going to get to Heaven, and one day Obadiah's going to walk up to us and we're going to get to talking, and he's going to ask us – how'd you like my book?" In this chapter, I'd like us to spend some time in Obadiah, mining it for the truths that God has entrusted to us. And maybe we'll be ready for that encounter with Obadiah in Heaven as well!

Obadiah lived in the early part of the 6th century B.C.E. Let's talk through a little background so we can place him correctly in the events of the Bible.

Moses led the people of Israel out of Egypt in approximately the 13th century before Christ. Joshua led them into the land of Israel, and they settled there over the next few centuries. During the time between the 13th and 11th centuries, we have the events recorded in the books of Joshua, Judges, and Ruth. In approximately 1040 B.C.E., Samuel anoints Saul to be the first king of Israel. Saul begins well, but he did not end well. He turns away from God and takes leadership on his own terms, so the kingdom is taken from him and given to a man after God's own heart, David. David reigns from approximately 1000 B.C.E. to 960 B.C.E. and is succeeded by his son Solomon. The time of David and Solomon is the golden age of Israel's history; never before and never again would Israel control the entirety of the land, conquer its foes, and find such prosperity and stability. Solomon dies in approximately 922 B.C.E., and due to poor leadership decisions by his son, Rehoboam, the nation splits into southern and northern kingdoms. The northern ten tribes secede from the nation and form the nation of Israel; the southern two tribes form the nation of Judah. The northern nation, Israel, does not follow the ways of God as prescribed in the Torah, the books of Moses; they do their own thing, getting involved in idolatry and wickedness that stuns the imagination. According to the biblical writers, there are no good kings in the northern nation; there is not one that follows God. God sends them prophet after prophet to communicate to them His love and His willingness to forgive if they will repent, turn from their wickedness, and return to Him, but they do not listen. So in His justice and love, God allows the nation of Assyria to come in 722 B.C.E. and destroy the northern nation of Israel. The people are deported from the land of promise, and they never return to constitute what was the northern nation.

The southern kingdom of Judah at times follows God, and at times not. There are good kings, like Hezekiah and Josiah, who provide godly leadership, and there are bad kings, like Manasseh, who don't. God sends prophets to help the people understand what He desires of them; He urges them to follow Him with all their hearts, and at times they do. But as time progresses, they do so less and less, and God promises that there will be judgment if they do not follow Him. That judgment arrives in the form of King Nebuchadnezzar and the nation of Babylon. Babylon attacks Judah and there are three battles, three victories by Babylon, and three deportations of the citizens of Judah: one in 605 B.C.E., one in 598 B.C.E., and one in 587/586 B.C.E. By 587/586, the Babylonians have lost patience with this wayward vassal state, and they decide to finish them off. Jerusalem and Solomon's Temple are both completely destroyed, and the people are deported into exile in Babylon.

Obadiah lived through the final days of Jerusalem. He would have been a witness to the majesty and glory of Solomon's Temple, and he would have seen the Babylonians come and destroy it.

The book of Obadiah is not about Babylon though. It's about Judah's neighbor to the southeast, the nation of Edom.

Edom was located southeast of the Dead Sea, its inhabitants descendants of Isaac's son Esau. They had never gotten along with the descendants of Isaac's other son Jacob, the people of Israel, from the days of the brothers until the days of Obadiah and beyond. You might remember from Genesis 27 that Jacob and Esau had a falling out, and though the two brothers were eventually reconciled, their descendants carried the feud on for the next two thousand years. Edom never liked their relatives in Israel, and at every opportunity they had to show it, they did.

When Moses and the people of Israel were coming from Egypt into the Promised Land, they requested to come through the territory of Edom; the Edomites refused them. We read their reply to Israel in Numbers 20 – **"you may not pass through here; if you try, we will march out and attack you with the sword."** Not the warmest of family greetings. If you get a reply like that to a Christmas card or family party invite, you might think twice about going for a visit!

When Babylon came to attack Jerusalem and sacked and destroyed it, what was Edom's response? Scripture records that the Edomites not only refused to assist the descendants of Jacob in their hour of greatest need, but instead stood by and watched as they were destroyed. They even assisted the Babylonians in ensuring that none of the people of Jerusalem escaped into the territory of Edom. They even helped plunder the city, taking for themselves what was never theirs, and they participated in the destruction of the city and the nation.

It is to this situation in this time that God speaks through the prophet Obadiah to the people of Edom and the people of Judah living in exile in Babylon.

Edom had watched and even participated in the destruction and murder of her neighbors and relatives to the north. The old blood feud had finally come to a point of culmination. The Old Testament scholar Costen Harrell says of the Edomites:

"Since the day when Jacob by cunning became possessor of his brother's birthright, the children of Esau and the children of Jacob had been on bad terms. Family feuds are long and bitter and tragic... the Edomites, like their father Esau, were a fleshly-minded people, having no appreciation of the unseen and no dreams for the future. They lived for food, spoil, and vengeance, with no national conscience or ideals. It is significant that nowhere in the Old Testament is any mention made of the gods of the Edomites. They doubtless had their gods, as other nations, but their deities must have been exceedingly drab and unappealing; for Israel, continually fascinated by the idolatries of her friends and foes, does not so much as intimate that Edom had a religion."[1]

We know very little of the man Obadiah, but we can see in his words that he was very hurt and angered by what he saw his neighbors and relatives doing to the people of Judah.

God spoke through Obadiah to what I believe is the very core issue of the Edomites: pride. Edom was well situated geographically to repel invaders and protect her territory. We know one of the cities of Edom quite well: the city of Petra. Images of this city were made popular in the third installment of the Indiana Jones movies. Petra was probably known then as Sela, the capital of Edom. Listen to the words of verse 3 and 4:

"'The pride of your heart has deceived you, you who live in the clefts of the rocks and make your home on the heights, you who say to yourself, 'Who can bring me down to the ground?' Though you soar like the eagle and make your nest among the stars, from there I will bring you down,' declares the Lord."

The people of Edom were absolutely secure in their own ability to protect themselves. They didn't need or want help from anyone, and they saw themselves as self-sufficient and superior to their kinsman to the north. Because they lived in the rock cities, they thought themselves invincible.

In verses 2-4, we see God telling Edom that He will make them "small among the nations" – that is, they will be insignificant. When you are as puffed up with pride as the people of Edom, that's quite a blow to the ego. God continues – "you will be utterly despised." Pride makes us susceptible to the opinions of others; we become experts at image management and reading the perceptions and approval of others. It has been said that the difference between politicians and statesmen is this very thing: do you care more about doing what is right, or do you can more about being liked? Edom was full of pride, and that pride caused her to act toward her relatives in Judah in a destructive and selfish way. Obadiah says that God will judge them for this.

Edom felt very secure trusting in her mountain fortresses, in her military might and prowess, and in her economic power. She was on a very important trading route, and she became a trading center of great power and prominence. The words of the psalmist ring in my ears here: **"some trust in chariots, and some in horses, but we trust in the name of the Lord our God."** Many people and nations throughout history have put their trust and their confidence in military might and economic power to protect them and preserve them, but each time the words of Scripture are proven true. True security and confidence can be found only in trusting in God. It is through Him and Him alone that we can find peace and security and confidence. Edom did not follow the words of the psalmist, and just like many nations today, chose instead to put her trust in her military might and economic power. God spoke to her and speaks to us today: don't make that mistake. Don't allow anything or anyone to take the place of God; our trust should be placed only in Him.

It seems clear both from the historical record and from the words of Obadiah that the Edomites sided with

Babylon, attempting to save herself from destruction and taking advantage of an opportunity to settle an old family feud. The people of Judah did not forget what they saw the Edomites doing in this terrible time of war and devastation, and God spoke through the prophet Obadiah that He saw their actions as well. They would be held accountable for what they had done.

The first takeaway I see for leaders from Obadiah is this: **Pride will always deceive and blind us.**

The people of Edom weren't dumb. They had seen nations come and go and had had numerous opportunities to strike back against the people of Judah. It was in Babylon's attack, though, that they saw an opportunity that they felt they had to take advantage of. They sided with the Babylonians, feeling sure that by doing so they would be preserving their nation. History records, though, that within forty years of the destruction of Jerusalem and Judah, the Babylonians would destroy the nation of Edom too. In the words of the ancient knight in the aforementioned Indiana Jones movie, they had "chosen poorly."

What blinded them to the truth that you cannot trust the Babylonians or any other ancient invaders? They were not a people given over to trust, as evidenced throughout Scripture by their animosity toward the people of Israel. Why decide to put their trust in their own military might and a partner like Babylon?

Simply this – pride will always deceive and blind us.

Pride makes us think that we are invincible, that we can never be brought down, that we are the greatest people in the greatest nation in the history of the world. Pride makes us think that the way things are today is the way they will always be, when a cursory reading of history tells us otherwise. Pride makes us trust in ourselves, in our own view of how things are and should be, when the Bible teaches us that we can trust and find our confidence only in God.

How many times as a leader have I fallen prey to this! And how many times have I seen others do so as well. Even in the midst of doing the work of God, it is easy to become prideful and begin to think more of ourselves than we ought. Edom is such a warning of the dangers of pride – to me and, I believe, to every other leader.

The people of Edom were blinded by their perception of their national security and military prowess, and they were blinded to the lunacy of trusting in a nation like Babylon. Edom placed her trust in what she had done, in her mountain fortresses and in her own wisdom. God spoke through the prophet Obadiah and told them of the folly of their actions.

Proverbs 16:18 says, **"Pride goes before destruction, a haughty spirit before a fall."** Pride will always bring us down. We see this in the history of nations and in the lives of individual leaders. Pride causes men, women, and nations to overreach and overpromise, and when reality intrudes on our pride, it can cause quite the crash.

What is the solution to pride? How can we avoid the danger that we see in the lives of the Edomites and throughout history? God has provided the solution for us – it is humility.

Proverbs 11:2 says, **"When pride comes, then comes disgrace, but with humility comes wisdom."**

When we seek to follow God with our whole hearts, with all our minds, souls, and strength, we learn the value of true humility and the danger of pride. In Scripture we see what happens when our pride takes over. We see it in the example of men like Uzziah, who was a great and powerful king of Judah who did so many good things but then decided that he knew better than God and disobeyed God's command. 2 Chronicles 26:16 tells us, **"But after Uzziah became powerful, his pride led to his downfall. He was unfaithful to the LORD his God, and entered the temple of the LORD to burn incense on the altar of incense."** He disobeyed God, and God struck him with leprosy as a reminder of his pride for the rest of his life. All the good that he had accomplished would not be remembered; what people would remember was that Uzziah was the king who had leprosy because he had disobeyed God.

When we repent of our pride – truly repent and turn away from the wickedness of trying to do things our own way – then Scripture says that God listens and hears us and forgives us. King Hezekiah of Judah learned this. We read in 2 Chronicles 32:26 about what happened when he turned back to God:

"Hezekiah repented of the pride of his heart, as did the people of Jerusalem; therefore the LORD's wrath did not come upon them during the days of Hezekiah. Hezekiah had very great riches and honor, and he made treasuries for his silver and gold and for his precious stones, spices, shields and all kinds of valuables. He also made buildings to store the harvest of grain, new wine and oil; and he made stalls for various kinds of cattle, and pens for the flocks. He built villages and acquired great numbers of flocks and herds, for God had given him very great riches. It was Hezekiah who blocked the upper outlet of the Gihon spring and channeled the water down to the west side of the City of David. He succeeded in everything he undertook."

Hezekiah repented of his pride and embraced humility, and God listened and blessed him and the nation of Judah for it.

The psalmist writes in Psalm 10:4- **"In his pride the wicked does not seek him; in all his thoughts there is no room for God."** This is why pride is so dangerous; it causes us to focus on ourselves and not on God. Pride makes us the king of our lives; it makes us the commander in chief of all that we are. Scripture, however, teaches that God is the source of all that is – that everything we are, everything we have, every part of our lives finds its source in God alone. We are simply stewards of the lives that God has given to us. I love my children so much, and whenever I am away from them I understand that in a fresh way, but I know that they are God's, and that he has only entrusted them to me. They are not mine – they are His, and He trusts me with them. It's when I forget that, when I start to think that I'm in charge, that my pride takes over and my focus on God diminishes.

Pride is what makes us have to be right in every discussion, in every argument, in every conversation. Pride is what makes a man feel that he must be the boss in his home instead of learning and living what the Bible teaches, that a marriage is two people who lovingly submit to each other (Ephesians 5:21), not one bossing the other around. Pride is what makes children stamp their feet and refuse to bend their will, even when they know inside what is the right thing to do. Pride is what makes adults stiff-necked and stubborn even when they know the right thing to do.

In short, pride is sin. Pride is refusing to submit to what God says is right and instead choosing our own way, our own preferences, our own knowledge over what God has revealed in the Bible.

Humility, on the other hand, is submission to what God says is right. Humility is seen in mutual submission in a marriage, putting the needs and wants of the other person ahead of your own. Humility is seen in loving others, in acknowledging that we don't know it all, in remaining teachable to all that God would show us through His Word and through others in our community of faith.

Humility is a huge part of having a heart for God and for people, just as Jesus told us to do.

Pride will always deceive us and blind us. Humility will set us free to love God and others as He intended. Two paths, not at all the same. The message of Obadiah 1-4 is this: choose humility. Choose God's way.

Scripture tells us that God is not mocked. He brings down the arrogant, if not in their lifetime, in their death and how history treats them. Lloyd Ogilvie tells the story of Louis XIV of France, who called himself "the great." He made the infamous assertion of pride, "I am the state!" His court was the most magnificent in Europe at that time. When he died, his funeral was spectacular. He had left behind orders to dramatize his greatness. He was placed in a gold coffin. The cathedral was dimly lit, with only one candle placed above his coffin. Thousands waited in hushed silence as Bishop Massilon was about to give an appropriate eulogy. Instead, slowly reaching down, he snuffed out the candle and said, "Only God is great."[2]

Louis XIV put his trust and his confidence in his own accomplishments; his pride was immense. The bishop spoke true words at his funeral, however; only God is great.

The Edomites missed this truth just as Louis did, and the consequences would be utter destruction. Edom faced destruction economically, they faced the loss of their wisdom and understanding, and they faced the loss of their military capability. All the things they were so proud of and all the things that they put their trust in – all were destroyed.

WHERE DOES THIS ROAD END?

While robbers and thieves usually only take items of value that they want, in God's judgment Edom would be completely plundered. Nothing would be left.

Did you know that grape harvesters don't pick every grape from the vines? There's only so long until the ripe grapes will go bad on the vine, so they must pick quickly. In the Mosaic Law, God told the people to leave some for the poor, the widow, and the orphan. Deuteronomy 24:19-21 says,

> **"When you are harvesting in your field and you overlook a sheaf, do not go back to get it. Leave it for the foreigner, the fatherless and the widow, so that the Lord your God may bless you in all the work of your hands. When you beat the olives from your trees, do not go over the branches a second time. Leave what remains for the foreigner, the fatherless and the widow. When you harvest the grapes in your vineyard, do not go over the vines again. Leave what remains for the foreigner, the fatherless and the widow."**

In the case of Edom, God says every grape will be gone; nothing will be left to them. Verse 6 says, **"But how Esau will be ransacked, his hidden treasures pillaged!"** The destruction will be complete. God says even what is hidden away will be found and will be pillaged.

Those whom you think you can trust will prove untrustworthy – you will have no allies. You will have no one you can depend on. Verse 7 says,

"All your allies will force you to the border; your friends will deceive and overpower you; those who eat your bread will set a trap for you, but you will not detect it."

The reference to "Those who eat your bread" refers to close friends who eat at your table with you. They will betray Edom.

And the wise men of Edom – those who have shared great wisdom with the people to provide for their economic and military security – they will be destroyed. Everything that the people have trusted in will be gone.

What have the people of Edom done to earn this? Verses 10-11 tell us – this judgment is earned. Their punishment has just cause.

"Because of the violence against your brother

Jacob, you will be covered with shame; you will be destroyed forever. On the day you stood aloof while strangers carried off his wealth and foreigners entered his gates and cast lots for Jerusalem, you were like one of them."

God is explaining their error to them, saying essentially, "You were not like a brother; you were not even like a good neighbor. You were like one of them, like one of the invading army of Babylon. It is because of your violence; it is because you stood aloof while your brothers were attacked; and it is because you took advantage of the situation."

The problem is not just their actions; it's their attitude of superior condescension and aloofness that God condemns them for.

The consequences of their actions are that they will be covered with shame; they will be destroyed forever. And so it was. History records that we do not hear again of the Edomites after the Babylonians attack them in the 6th century B.C.E. They are wiped out, and it will be like they never existed. They will be treated as they treated Judah: they participated in the "cutting off" or destruction of Judah; God will cut them off. They will be utterly extirpated. God will treat them as they treated His people.

We read in Psalm 137:7 and Ezekiel 35:13 about the cries of the Edomites in these days regarding the destruction of Jerusalem by Babylon: "tear it down, they cried, tear it down to its foundations!" Not only did they rejoice because of what had happened to the people of Jerusalem and Judah, but they had given aid to and actively assisted their persecutors! This was not something that was overlooked by God; the prophet Obadiah conveys that He has seen and heard what has happened, and He will deal with them appropriately.

My takeaway for leaders from this passage is simple: **pride leads us to destruction.**

It was because of the pride of the Edomites that they trusted Babylon and allied with her against the people of Judah. It was because of their pride that they took advantage of the situation and assisted in the plundering and destruction of the city of Jerusalem. It was because of their pride that they gloated and boasted over the fall of their relatives to the north, the people of Judah. And pride will not go unpunished by God.

The minute we think we know better than God, the minute we think that we can trust in anything other than Him, we become guilty of the same sin as the Edomites. And if we do not repent of it, turn from it, and embrace God and His ways, we will face the same judgment: destruction. Our spiritual lives will become dry and dusty; our lives on this earth will lack meaning and purpose. We will not know what it is to live in the pleasure of God; instead, we will seek to please ourselves and will, therefore, please neither God nor ourselves.

Pride will lead us to destruction. Sometimes that destruction will be revealed in what we do, and sometimes it will be revealed in our relationships. Can you think of a time when a refusal to admit you were wrong damaged a relationship with a co-worker, supervisor, or subordinate? How about with a spouse or child? A parent or a sibling?

Pride can lead to the damaging or even destruction of relationships.

How we treat our brothers and sisters matters to God. How we treat other lives that He has created matters to Him. Scripture is abundantly clear on this issue; every life matters to God, and if we are not actively involved in helping others, we are not obeying the two greatest commandments as given by Jesus: loving God with all our hearts, souls, minds, and strength, and loving our neighbor as we love ourselves. Jesus said the second was like the first; they are intertwined. Loving God cannot be correctly done without loving others, and vice versa.

Israel may have wondered if God had noticed what was going on; the prophecy of Obadiah would have put an end to those feelings of abandonment. God is sovereign. We see this truth throughout the pages of Scripture, and the prophet Obadiah communicates that clearly here. God is Lord of history, Lord of all nations, and He will punish sin. There are no free passes. Paul writes in Romans 6:23 that the wages of sin is death, separation from God, now and forever. But thank God for His love! Paul writes also that the gift of God is eternal life through Jesus Christ our Lord. When we choose to follow Jesus, to become his disciple and follow His ways and not our own, when we repent of our sin and turn from it, He will accept us and clothe us with His righteousness, that we would not perish but instead find eternal, abundant life as God intended it.

Pride leads to destruction, to death, just as all sin does; humbling ourselves to accept the gift of grace and reconciliation with God that He alone offers us leads to life. Leaders, I pray that is a decision and commitment that you have made. I pray that you are not trapped in the sin of the Edomites, the sin of pride, believing that the way of the world and those around you leads to life. Pride will lead us to destruction every time.

HOW DO WE CONQUER PRIDE?

The Day of the Lord was a term that the prophets used to refer to that time when justice would be done, when God would set things right, rewarding the righteous and punishing the wicked. The people of Israel and Judah looked forward to this day, but the prophets time and again told them that they shouldn't look forward to it quite so much, that they were, indeed, sinners who had earned the judgment of God.

Obadiah tells the people that the day of the Lord – this great day of reckoning and justice – is near. He goes on to cite the law of just recompense; just as you have done, so it will be done to you. Your deeds will return on your own head.

The Edomites had turned against their relatives to the north, the nation of Judah. They had joined with the Babylonians in their destruction of Jerusalem and the Temple, and they had hunted down fugitives trying to escape from the Babylonian army and had turned them in. God says through the prophet Obadiah that their actions will come back home to roost. They will pay for what they have done, and the punishment will fit the crime. God will repay them for what they did to His chosen people. He will treat Edom as they treated others, and their punishment will be especially harsh because they did evil on holy ground, the city of Jerusalem.

In Scripture, we see different images associated with punishment from God. Obadiah uses the imagery of drinking: punishment from God is said to be like drinking the cup of God's wrath. We see similar imagery in multiple places, mostly in the book of Revelation and in those of the prophets. We also see the imagery of a cup of punishment for sin in the Garden of Gethsemane when Jesus asked that this "cup" pass from Him if it were possible.

Obadiah speaks of the nations violating God's holy place, and their punishment is that they will "drink continually" from the cup of God's wrath; they will drink and drink and be as if they had never been. They had destroyed Jerusalem, but Jerusalem would rise again; the punishment of the Edomites would result in complete destruction; it would be as if they had never existed. The Day of the Lord – the day of judgment – would turn things around from how they seemed.

The people of Edom were gloating and prideful; they needed to hear the message of judgment that Obadiah was bringing.

The people of Judah were devastated; they needed to hear the message of hope that Obadiah was bringing.

I believe verse 17 is the key verse in this book – **"But on Mount Zion will be deliverance; it will be holy, and the house of Jacob will possess its inheritance."**

In Obadiah we do indeed see words of hope: on Mount Zion will be deliverance. There is still hope; God is not done with His people. Again Mount Zion will be holy. Again the people will worship God there, and the house of Jacob will possess its inheritance.

The people heard this message and their minds were drawn to the restoration of the land. The land was tied in their minds to the blessing of God; if they had the land, God was blessing them. If they were in exile, God was punishing them. The land was everything. That's why in the Hebrew Bible, the order of the books is different from the order of the Protestant Bible. Second Chronicles ends the Hebrew Bible with the decree of Cyrus that allowed the Jewish exiles to return to the land and worship their God in their way. The return to the land was HUGE to them, and that's why for two thousand years after the destruction of Jerusalem and the Temple again in 70 A.D., every year at Passover the Jewish people have said, "next year in Jerusalem" – the promise of the land is important because it signifies that God is with them and is blessing them.

As I read Obadiah though, something else comes to my mind. When I read that the house of Jacob will possess its inheritance, I think of a promise that was given to Abraham, Isaac, and Jacob back in Genesis, a promise that is the greatest part of their inheritance, much more significant than the land. Genesis 12:3 – **"all peoples on earth will be blessed through you"** and Genesis 28:14 - **"All peoples on earth will be blessed through you and your offspring."** We read those promises made to Abraham and Jacob and we understand them to be promises not only of land, but also of a blessing in which all people can partake: the blessing of Messiah, the one who would come and offer reconciliation with God to all who would believe and accept Him.

So when I read in Obadiah "the house of Jacob will possess its inheritance," that's what I think of; that's the inheritance that I believe God is speaking of through the prophet Obadiah. I think he is speaking here of the promise of the One who would come, Jesus the Messiah. Six centuries in advance, God is reiterating that His promise will be fulfilled; He will keep His word, just as He spoke it to Abraham and Jacob some twelve hundred years before Obadiah.

On Mount Zion there would be deliverance. The ultimate deliverance of all sinners would come through the cross of Calvary where Jesus was murdered, where He suffered and died for your sin and mine. On Mount Zion there would be deliverance; the sin would be covered and reconciliation with God would be made possible. We would be delivered from the just consequences of our sin, an eternity in hell separated from God. On Mount Zion there would be deliverance, and it would be holy. Mount Zion would be set apart from all other places on earth because it was in this place that God would redeem through the blood of Jesus all those who would bow the knee to Him and accept the gift of the Messiah, the one promised by God Himself as the inheritance of Abraham, Isaac, and Jacob.

Verse 18 speaks of the ultimate disposition of the people of Judah and the people of Edom:

"the house of Jacob will be a fire and the house of Joseph a flame; the house of Esau will be stubble, and they will set it on fire and consume it. There will be no survivors from the house of Esau. The Lord has spoken."

Fire is used as a symbol of God's judgment in Scripture; here we see that the house of Jacob and house of Joseph (another way to speak of God's people in Israel and Judah) would survive and would in fact be used on the Day of the Lord as tools in God's hand to punish other sinful nations, including Edom.

Of Edom, God says there would be no survivors. Their sin is such that they have been offered time to repent but they refused, so their punishment will be complete destruction. If they had turned from their pride and their sin, if they had repented and turned back to God, He would have heard and would have forgiven them, just as He promises in His Word to do for all who turn from their sin and turn to Him. But Edom's pride would not allow her to bend the knee, so punishment came.

Verses 19 and 20 tell us that God's people will reclaim the Promised Land, from Dan to Beersheba. The land will be restored! That promise had to sound so good to the people who were living in exile in Babylon. Punishment would last for a while, but restoration would happen. And the book concludes with verse 21 – **"Deliverers will go up on Mount Zion to govern the mountains of Esau, and the kingdom will be the Lord's."**

The book ends with the ultimate promise: the kingdom will be the Lord's. He will reign supreme in the end, and everything will be set right. He is sovereign. The new day will be different from all those that had gone before; this time God will be king and His reign will have no end. We know the end of the book: God rules.

As I read the prophecy of Obadiah, I am reminded of several truths.

First, the day of judgment and reckoning is near. Edom saw its day of judgment not long after these words were penned. All of humanity faces a day of judgment and reckoning. We will all face God and will have to own what we have done. Scripture says that all have sinned and that we all fall short of the glory of God. We all stand accused before the holiness of God. And we don't know when that day will come for each of us; for some it could be this very day.

Obadiah is using Edom as an object lesson for the people of Judah. "See them – see what they are facing because of their sin? See how their pride made them think that they would never face consequences for their sin? Learn from this! Don't follow their example – follow God!"

Edom becomes a teaching example that Obadiah uses for the exiles from Jerusalem and Judah and for us as well. We have to bear in mind that each day could be our last; today could be the day that we stand before God. Are we prepared for that possibility? Are we ready to meet our Creator and Judge?

God's judgment is universal. It is not only His people who face His judgment; it is all mankind. And there is only one way to be ready: that is through the work and power of Jesus Christ. Because of what Jesus our Messiah did, we can accept His righteousness to cover our sin. We can stand righteous before God, not because of ourselves or what we have done, but because of what Jesus did. We can stand holy before Him, not because we are holy in our own right, but because Jesus is holy and He clothes us with His righteousness and holiness. We simply must accept that gift from God, the gift of life, eternal salvation from what we deserve, starting today and lasting forever. Obadiah communicates this truth: the day of judgment and reckoning is near. Are we prepared? We can be, but only by accepting Jesus as our Savior and Lord. It is only in Him that we can find salvation and life. Jesus said in John 14:6 – **"I am the way, the truth, and the life – and no one comes to the Father except through me."**

Second, we might think we understand situations and circumstances at times, but in fact God has something else in mind. The people who first heard Obadiah's message saw the possession of their inheritance to mean the possession of the land of Israel; I think God was referring to their ultimate inheritance of the promises to the patriarchs, the provision of Jesus the Messiah for the sin of all who would accept Him and believe.

It is so important to be teachable and to have a humble spirit, especially when we come to the Word of God. If we come with our preconceived ideas, it is very likely that we will come away with an interpretation that fits what we want it to say. That's what I believe happened in the case of verse 17 (**"Jacob will possess his inheritance"**). If, though, we come to the text and ask God to speak to us and teach us what He wants us to see and hear, I believe that He will and that we will learn so much more than we can imagine. The key is a humble and teachable heart. We have to be willing to change some of our preconceived ideas. We have to be willing to listen to God and learn from His Word.

Third, we can find comfort and hope in the knowledge that God will make all things right in His way and in His time. The people of Judah needed to hear this message; they were in exile and needed the message of hope that God had not forgotten them and that they were still valued in His eyes. We need to hear that same message. Every life matters to God – yours and mine and every other one. God will make all things right; His justice is sure.

Scripture tells us that vengeance is God's, not ours, to take; we are to forgive. This was a hard thing for the people of Judah to do. They didn't like hearing that message any more than we do at times. But Obadiah taught them that they needed to learn from the example of Edom what not to do. They needed to forgive others so that God would forgive them.

Jesus said that we should treat others the way we want to be treated and do to others as we want to have done to us. How we treat others, what we do and say to them, demonstrates our salvation (or its lack). We are called to love others as God has loved us. We are challenged to rely on God's ultimate justice, and by doing that we demonstrate our faith in God in real, visible ways.

Even when it's hard, even when we struggle, we need to practice the compassion and forgiveness of God because we trust Him and because He tells us to do so. It's a matter of obedience. We have to live by the standards that God presents in His Word. We have to trust Him that He will make things right in His way and in His time.

Simon Wiesenthal tells of facing this choice in his book *The Sunflower.* As a young Polish soldier in World War II, he watched helplessly as German soldiers killed his grandmother and then forced his mother into a freight car filled with elderly Jewish women. Eventually Wiesenthal would count eighty-nine relatives who were killed by the Nazis.

One day on a prison detail in a Nazi hospital, Wiesenthal received a summons. A nurse signaled him to accompany her up a stairway and down a hallway to where a lone Nazi soldier lay swathed in bandages.

In that musty hospital room, the soldier compelled Wiesenthal to listen to his story. He said, "I must tell you of this horrible deed – tell you because you are a Jew." Long separated from the lifestyle and faith of his church upbringing, he found his military attachment in battle in a village in the Ukraine. Booby traps killed 30 members of his unit. In revenge, this soldier and his squad herded three hundred Jews into a three-story house, doused it with gasoline, and fired grenades into it. Drawn guns ensured that no one escaped.

The wounded soldier said to Wiesenthal, "I am left here with my guilt. In the last hours of my life you are with me. I do not know who you are. I know only that you are a Jew and that is enough. In the long nights while I have been waiting for death, time and time again I have longed to talk about it to a Jew and beg forgiveness from him. I know what I am asking is almost too much for you, but without your answer I cannot die in peace."

Simon Wiesenthal stared out the window at the sunlit courtyard, looked at the bandaged soldier lying in the bed, and without a word left the room. That decision haunted him the remainder of his life.[3]

I've heard that unforgiveness is like drinking poison and expecting the other person to die. Forgiveness seems unfair – it seems unjust – but God says in His Word that it is godly. Forgiveness extended in Jesus' name is what we are called as followers of Jesus to be always willing to offer, always willing to extend to all who would ask us, even when and especially when it's hard and from our perspective undeserved. Forgiveness is a natural outgrowth of humility, of understanding who we are and whose we are, that we belong to God and that we are His possession.

My takeaway for leaders from this passage is this: **Pride <u>can</u> be conquered with a proper focus on God.**

It is through a focus on God that we understand our proper place and size in the grand scheme of things. We understand that we are servants of the most High, just like Obadiah, that we can boast only in Him and what He has done, never in ourselves and what we have done. We are sinners saved by grace. It is in grateful humility that we live, always willing to share the grace and forgiveness that we have received from God with other people. How can one who has been forgiven so much refuse to offer forgiveness to another? Scripturally speaking, we cannot.

I pray that this would be true of every leader, that we would live our lives committed to humbly serving others. I pray that every leader will strive to have a teachable spirit at all times in order to learn from God and from those He puts around us in our community of faith and in our lives.

PRINCIPLES FROM OBADIAH:

- Pride will always deceive and blind us.
- Pride leads us to destruction.
- Pride <u>can</u> be conquered with a proper focus on God.

5 HAGGAI

"Now this is what the Lord Almighty says: '"Give careful thought to your ways."'
--Haggai 1:5

Get to work.

That is a major theme of the prophets, including one whose prophecy we'll tackle in this chapter, Haggai.

Who was Haggai? His name means "festal or festival." That could mean that he was born during one of the three pilgrimage feasts of the Jews (Unleavened Bread, Pentecost or Weeks, and Tabernacles). Only his title is given; there's no family statement (whom he's the son of).

Except for Obadiah, Haggai is the shortest book in the Old Testament, made up of just thirty-eight verses in two chapters, and his book is among the most precisely dated in the entire Old Testament. The first message was delivered on the first day of the sixth month; that would be August 29 on our calendar, in the year 520 B.C.E. His last message was delivered on the twenty-fourth day of the ninth month; that would be December 18 on our calendar, in the same year. The entirety of his recorded ministry lasted just four months – really, really short compared to the other prophets – but what an effect it had.

Haggai was the first prophet after the exile to Babylon, and his ministry took place after Obadiah's. The people of Judah have been in exile in Babylon since the destruction of Jerusalem and the Temple in 587/586 B.C.E. Thanks to a decree from Cyrus the king of Persian (who had conquered the Babylonians) in 538 B.C.E., the people of Israel were permitted to travel home and worship as they chose. About fifty thousand Israelites made the decision to leave Babylon and travel back home. They arrived and began rebuilding, and what a task it was. They started work on rebuilding the Temple, getting the altar built and the foundation laid, but they faced a great deal of opposition from the neighboring peoples, so much so that they chose to stop work. And for nearly twenty years, the Temple rebuilding was at a standstill.

Why did they let it go so long? Wasn't it important to them?

The problems, as diagnosed by Haggai and others, were two: spiritual lethargy and apathy. Resignation to the way things were and apathy about whether things would ever get better had killed the faith of the people in the land.

We don't know how old Haggai was when he began speaking to the people. Many scholars believe that he was older. Haggai 2:3 says, **"Who of you is left who saw this house in its former glory? How does it look to you now? Does it not seem to you like nothing?"** If that verse implies that Haggai had seen Solomon's temple sixty-six years prior, he would obviously have been older, but we can't be sure. Based on 2:3, I tend to think Haggai was indeed an older man who had see the first Temple.

Haggai has been called the most matter-of-fact of all the prophets. Along with another prophet named Zechariah, he encouraged the returned exiles to refocus their priorities on God and His work.

During the time of Haggai, Darius the Great, also called Darius Hystaspes (not to be confused with Darius the Mede or Darius the Persian), ruled Persia, the greatest superpower in history up through this time, from 522-486 B.C.E. Incidentally, Darius was the king who ordered the trilingual inscription to be carved on the Behistun cliff wall (located in modern day Iran). By studying this inscription that was written in Akkadian, Elamite, and Old Persian, modern scholars were able to translate cuneiform, enabling us today to understand the culture and history of ancient Mesopotamia as never before.

We begin the book with Haggai's speaking on the first day of the month. This was socially an important day, at times occasioned by special offerings and sacrifice, celebration, and rejoicing (Numbers 10:10; 28:11-15).

However, with no temple, they couldn't do all that.

Haggai opens by saying that the word of the Lord came to Haggai. That's a common way of showing the true source of the message of this book, God. It's a statement of authority, just as we see in the books of Jeremiah, Ezekiel, Joel, Jonah, Micah, Zephaniah, Hosea, Zechariah, and Malachi. It is emphasized a little more here though; four times in five verses we hear that this is a message from God through His servant, the prophet Haggai.

The message of Haggai was addressed to the governor and the high priest, the civil and religious leaders of the restored Jewish community. Haggai recognized the leadership that was in place and addressed the message to the leaders first.

In some Bible versions, you might see the Hebrew translated Lord Almighty; in some it's translated Lord of Hosts. This name of God in Hebrew stresses the might, the power, and the sovereignty of God; this title is used more than ninety times in Haggai, Zechariah, and Malachi (fourteen times in Haggai alone). It can mean human armies (e.g. Exodus 7:4, Psalm 44:9), the celestial bodies (sun, moon, stars) (e.g. Deuteronomy 4:19, Isaiah 40:26), or angels (e.g. Joshua 5:14, 1 Kings 22:19, Psalm 148:2). This title for God is perhaps best understood as a general reference to the sovereignty of God over all powers in the universe.

Apparently some among the returned exiles had been saying that the time was not yet ripe to rebuild the Temple despite the fact that the people had returned to the land nearly twenty years prior. And God's message has to do with that very thing. He begins by referring to their message, and refers to them as "these people."

Uh oh. Notice it's "these people," not "my people." Here we see a phrase reflecting judgment and distancing.

Remember that I said the people had begun to rebuild the Temple but had faced opposition so they stopped? What I think Haggai's saying here is this: "I hear you saying with your actions and your words that you don't really care if God is with us; obedience is optional. You talk of when we get living conditions and the economy right, and when we develop a decent standard of living, and when we negotiate proper wage rates, and when we get the kids through school, and when life finally slows down, **then** there will be time for religion and God. We'll get to it... eventually... when the time is right..."

For nearly twenty years, they've been putting this off, procrastinating while they focused on their own homes and worked on their own lives. I like how Alec Motyear puts it: Haggai's point is that "the Lord does not tolerate a society run on these lines. He is not a complacent on-looker; He will be central or He will be at odds."[1]

The people had been making decisions that focused first on their own needs and wants and then offering to God what was left over after matters of personal security and comfort had first been decided. This is **not** the path of authentic disciples.

Understand – this is not about the Temple building. Not building the temple was not the problem; it was merely a symptom. The problem was much deeper: an uncommitted life.

Motyear again says: "The house was the outward form of the real presence of the Lord among them. To refuse to build the house was at best saying that it did not matter whether the Lord was present with them. At worst, it was presuming on divine grace, that the Lord would live with His people even though they willfully refused to fulfill the condition of His indwelling that He had laid down. It amounted to seeking grace but refusing the means of grace… the important thing was not the size or the magnificence of the house, but the existence of it - that they want the indwelling God among them."[2]

They verbally might have articulated a belief to the contrary, but their actions spoke quite loudly of their misplaced priorities.

Haggai refers to their "paneled houses." This was cedar paneling, usually connected with royal dwellings (you'll find it in the descriptions of Solomon's palace and the first Temple). He's pointing out that the people have given attention to their own houses, but not to God's. Money was no obstacle for their getting to the finishing and decorative stage on their own homes, but they haven't even gotten the structure of the Temple rebuilt! There is some measure of affluence seen here; they've been able to do in their private homes what Solomon had done in the temple and the palace. They were not destitute; as we read in a few verses, they had seed to sow, food to eat, wine to drink, clothes to wear, and gainful employment, but no true satisfaction.

Haggai's telling them that they have lost their enthusiasm for the work of God.

He gives them some good advice, and this is the first principle from Haggai that I'd suggest for leaders: **Give careful thought to your ways.** "Your ways" are your conduct, your actions, and their consequences. In the book of Haggai, we'll eventually see this counsel repeated four times (1:5, 1:7; 2:15, 2:18).

He's talking about a total re-orientation and re-organization of priorities in the lives of the people. God is to be first. Those who put God's Kingdom and righteousness before their own material needs will find these needs supplied as well (Matthew 6:25-33).

What are the people supposed to do? Rethink, reexamine, reorder, and refocus. I think it's helpful to ask the question: to what is my life committed?

For me, I see it like this: my first commitment is to Jesus Christ, my Lord and Savior. After that, I am committed to my wife, Charlotte; then to my children, and then to God's church. That order is very important; we've all seen families derailed and lives devastated by getting that order wrong.

Too many people in our day say their kids are the priority in their lives, and their calendar and checkbooks reflect that. The problem with that line of thinking is that according to Biblical priorities, children are to come third, not first; God is to come first, followed by your spouse, and then your kids.

How many marriages have imploded because children were placed at a higher priority than the marriage relationship? This is a dangerous road to walk, and leaders are not immune to getting their priorities out of whack. Have you ever seen a leader so consumed with work that they neglect time with their spouse and children? How about a pastor who is so consumed with the work of ministry that he or she neglects time with God to do it? These examples and scores more are as real in our day as they were in Haggai's, and just as dangerous.

Haggai's intent is to pull people out of their preoccupation with their own stuff and work together for the Kingdom I think a good question for leaders to ask themselves is this: am I too busy to serve God or support His work? To what is my life **really** committed? In my life, where is the priority of the Glory of God?

Remember: God doesn't save people just to save them. He always has a purpose in mind for His people. And obedience to God is not optional for those who seek to follow Him with all their hearts, souls, minds, and strength.

The problem for the people of Haggai's audience was not the building; it was the heart. How important are the things of God to us? What are our priorities?

It's always helpful for me to do a radical self-examination of my life, my priorities, and my commitments. I'd highly recommend that exercise for you as well.

What that might mean is that you stop doing some things, or that you start doing some things, or both. And that's ok.

I remember in 2006 that there was a time of Q&A with the members of the Southview before they called me into the lead pastor role. One question from that Q&A stands out to this day in my mind. Someone asked, "Will you start doing new things? And will you stop doing some of what we're currently doing?" My answer: "Absolutely." That's part of what it means to follow God: to listen to His voice and follow where He leads. That always involves change whether it's an individual, a church, a family, or an organization.

In Isaiah 43:18-19, we read, **"Forget the former things; do not dwell on the past. See, I am doing a**

**new thing! Now it springs up; do you not perceive
it?"** A <u>new</u> thing!

What is the new thing that God is calling *you* to? What
has He uniquely equipped and gifted and called *you* to do?
What does he have in store for *you*?

In his book *Chazown*, Craig Groeschel talks about finding that unique thing. He talks about the intersection of
three areas: your spiritual gifts, your core values, and your
past experiences. Where those three meet, there is a sweet
spot, and that's where you have the opportunity to be
what God wired you to be.

There is a job to do in our day. God's work demands
your and my best energy, your and my best efforts, and
your and my complete commitment. That requires a self-
assessment. I have to know where I am first; then I can
focus on where I need to go and what I need to do.

Before you dig any further into Haggai, spend some
time doing that self-assessment, and see what comes out

of that. Don't just do it in your head; put it on paper, and take a good, hard look at where you are.

A PROPER PERSPECTIVE

Haggai continues in verse 6 with language strikingly reminiscent of Deuteronomy 28 and Leviticus 26, where Moses told the people of the blessings of following God's way and the curses of disobeying. Grain and corn were harvested at the end of May or the beginning of June, and Haggai is addressing the people here at the end of August. The disappointing harvest of the last season is still fresh in their minds. They have a "purse full of holes" – that means that prices are high and buying power is low. Inflation is rampant, and there's no end in sight. Haggai tells them that this is a sign; it is the unfruitfulness of a land judged by God, and it will result in futility in all that they try to do.

What they are experiencing is the result of a failure to keep the covenant. All of these illustrations speak of the difficulties that happen to a people who have not included God in their plans and in their lives, and who are preoccupied with their own self-interests. The people's perspectives have become skewed. Haggai wants them to stop, take stock, and evaluate.

He tells them that God will take pleasure in obedience! He will be honored by a nation that follows His ways, and they will see fruit from that choice. But instead, they're all busy with their own houses, running to and fro and trying to get more done, get better results, and make things happen the way they want. Sound familiar to you at all?

In verse 11, God calls for a drought; that's serious business to an agricultural people. That's not all, either; a drought often signifies a coming famine. The Hebrew word here is hareb (drought), similar to the word horeb (ruin). The <u>drought</u> and the Temple's <u>ruin</u> are connected; he's making a play on words here to get the people to connect the two.

Grain, new wine, and oil were the three basic crops of the land. These three are often mentioned in the context of God's blessing or cursing of the land based on the obedience or disobedience of the people (e.g. Deuteronomy 7:13, Joel 1:10). Olive oil was especially valuable, as it was used as food, fuel for lights, and medicine.

The drought would affect people and cattle, signifying that the consequences of sin affect all of creation; nothing is going to thrive during this time of discipline because of the people's disobedience. Nothing will be excluded from the effects of this discipline. God is sovereign over all of creation. The Bible speaks of His control over the natural elements and the agricultural cycle, one of the reasons God is called by the title "Lord Almighty" or "Lord of Hosts" fourteen times in this book.

Robert Alden says, "Throughout the Bible it is clear that all of creation suffers because of the sin of man - it would appear that the happiness and productivity of creation depends on the relationship of man to God and man to man."[3] Sin and disobedience have consequences.

Haggai is communicating to the people that their circumstances – the drought, the coming famine, and the high inflation – are consequences of their disobedience. God had said that disobedience would have a price, and that's what they are seeing, but they are not interpreting it correctly. Haggai is helping them to see through the lens of godliness; this is divine discipline, not just a couple of bad harvest years.

Part of the blessing God promised to his people was that they would eat and be satisfied. Deuteronomy 6:10-12 says,

> **"When the Lord your God brings you into the land he swore to your fathers, to Abraham, Isaac and Jacob, to give you—a land with large, flourishing cities you did not build, houses filled with all kinds of good things you did not provide, wells you did not dig, and vineyards and olive groves you did not plant—then when you eat and are satisfied, be careful that you do not forget the Lord, who brought you out of Egypt, out of the land of slavery."**

But the reverse would apply to the curse for disobedience; they would eat and not be satisfied. Leviticus 26:26 says,

"When I cut off your supply of bread, ten women will be able to bake your bread in one oven, and they will dole out the bread by weight. You will eat, but you will not be satisfied."

God had demonstrated His faithfulness to the covenant by bringing the Jews into favor with Cyrus, who permitted them to return home and rebuild their temple; he even supplied the resources to do so! The people were supposed to demonstrate their faithfulness to God by rebuilding the Temple, but they messed up. They didn't do it, and they didn't make any plans to do it. They procrastinated while they went about building their own homes and worrying about their own lives. And by rejecting their responsibility to the covenant with God, they invited His judgment, just as He had promised in Deuteronomy and Leviticus.

In our day, we talk a lot about the love of God, and rightly so. God's love is unfathomable, and we could spend every day for all of eternity exploring the height and depth of it. But if we're not careful, we can emphasize the love of God to the complete exclusion of the wrath and judgment of God; we do that to our peril. God is full of love and mercy, but He is also just; Scripture says that He disciplines those whom He loves. And the people of Israel were told, under the old covenant, that they could and should evaluate their circumstances in light of their level of obedience to Him.

Haggai wants the people to consider and give thought to their ways so that they can come to the correct conclusions. They must see their circumstances from the point of view of what God wants from them. He wants to remind the people that their relationship with God affects EVERYTHING.

They knew the Law and the Prophets, and they should have connected the dots here, but they had not considered their current circumstances from this perspective because they were too wrapped up in their own affairs.

Under the terms of the covenant that God made with Abraham and codified under Moses, Haggai is explaining to the people that their economic circumstances are closely related to their spiritual circumstances. Abundance was one of the blessings of God to the people when they obeyed the Law. This does not translate into our day because we are under the new covenant, not the old. We are not bound to the Law of Moses; we are free in Christ! We cannot take this principle from the Old Testament and use it to teach or believe that the godly person will necessarily become prosperous from a material and financial point of view. I think there is, though, basis for the belief that prosperity cannot bring happiness and contentment to those who do not put God first in their lives.

For the people in Haggai's day, we have to be careful to understand this correctly. Blessing would not <u>always</u> be the reward for obedience, and curse could not <u>always</u> be traced to disobedience (think about Job and all that he went through). The experience of hardship and suffering in life may be linked to disobedience and God's discipline, but there could be other reasons as well.

The prophet is not saying or suggesting that every experience of suffering or hardship in our lives is automatically to be seen as a sign of God's discipline. The point here is we have to see that as a possibility and examine ourselves to see if our current circumstances are related to our current obedience level. God's discipline of His people, just like church discipline, is never punitive punishment; it is always to bring us back to a right relationship with Him. Always.

Mark Boda puts it this way: "In light of the teaching of Scripture, experiences of hardship should always become opportunities for spiritual reflection in our lives, turning us heavenward to ask hard questions… such questions of God should be accompanied by questions directed inward as we ask God to search us for those areas that do not reflect the priorities of the kingdom (Psalm 139)."[4]

There is hope. No matter where we've been or what we've done, there is hope; but we must choose to change. If we do - if we turn away from our disobedience and return to God - He will accept us as He has promised.

There could have been no restoration of the relationship of the people of God to Him if there had been no repentance. They had to turn away from their disobedient ways and begin to obey the Word of God. Their hearts had to change and their actions had to reflect that change. They had to acknowledge their past choices that were wrong and they had to change, starting that day. That doesn't mean that they have to be perfect and get their lives all straightened out before they come to God – if that were the case, they'd never come to God! Haggai is pointing them to the fact that they must turn away from trusting in themselves and turn to trusting in God alone. They have to make that choice – no one else can make it for them.

My takeaway for leaders is this: **A proper perspective is pivotal.**

We can look at our circumstances in two ways: the natural view and the godly view.

Pieter Verhoeff says, "Throughout history, Israel and then the Church has tended toward the natural view - this is just how things are. The prophet Haggai reminds us to evaluate our lives and our circumstances in the light of the Word of God and to seek first His Kingdom and His righteousness (Matthew 6:33) Looking from the [godly] perspective can help us to understand that our current "drought" or whatever is happening in our situation, could be God's discipline for our waywardness, apathy, and negligence in committing ourselves to serve the Lord and build His Kingdom."[5]

As leaders, we help people set perspective. How we lead, what we say, what we do – all that can contribute toward a perspective either centered on God or centered on us and our circumstances. To get the right perspective, it's critical for leaders to pull aside, to evaluate, and to "consider our ways" as Haggai has already taught us. Leaders set the tone, and if we set a godly perspective, those we lead will take note.

I've seen this to be true more times than I can count in my own leadership. In a church setting, people look to the pastors to help them set perspective, to teach them how to develop a proper outlook on the events in life. They may not always ask, and they may not always like what they hear, but our responsibility as leaders is to help them in this. It begins, though, with our own perspective.

We can never lead someone farther than we have gone ourselves.

THE RESPONSE

How did the people respond to Haggai?

Verse 12 tells us –

"Then Zerubbabel son of Shealtiel, Joshua son of Jozadak, the high priest, and the whole remnant of the people obeyed the voice of the Lord their God and the message of the prophet Haggai, because the Lord their God had sent him."

They humbled themselves and acted in obedience to the Word of God. They saw their sin and responded appropriately.

And how did God respond to their obedience?

He affirmed the covenant relationship with His people. He told them "I am with you." Is there anything better than that? Theologian E. B. Pusey says, "All the needs and longings of the creature are summed up in these words - I am with you."[6]

Verse 14 tells us that God stirred the spirit of the leaders and the remnant. You can also translate that "moved the heart."

God is involved throughout this process:

- He raised up the Persian king Cyrus and the nation of Persia and allowed Israel to return to the land
- He raised up two godly leaders, Zerubbabel and Joshua
- He sent the prophet Haggai to the people
- He stirred the spirits of the leaders and the remnant
- He renewed His promise to be with them

Zechariah 4:6 says, **"not by might, nor by power, but by my spirit says the Lord."**

The people see and hear here that the covenant with God is still in force, that there is continuity with the past, that there is forgiveness for the present, and that there is hope for the future. God is *always* ready to affirm His covenant and bless His people when they choose obedience, but they must choose to listen and to obey.

Answer the questions below for yourself as we close out chapter one of Haggai.

Now that we've spent some time evaluating our priorities and our current situation and circumstances, what areas do you need to focus on to grow in your obedience to God and His Word?

What is the next step in your plan to grow in this area? To be intentional, plan with the end in mind, but plan some steps or benchmarks between you and your goal.

What steps can you take this week to grow in your obedience to what God is asking of you?

WE'RE NOT DONE YET...

All's well that ends well, right? Well, we're not done with Haggai quite yet.

The book continues with another statement similar to its opening, introducing the second prophetic speech or sermon of Haggai, but this time it's a month and a half later. The twenty-first day of the seventh month was the last day of the Feast of Tabernacles, a celebration that God had commanded His people to observe. It was a time when the entire nation would move out of their homes and live in booths, or "tabernacles" – temporary structures – when they would remember God's provision to the people of Israel in the wilderness during the Exodus and God's protection of His people. It was to be a time of thankfulness, for the harvest specifically, but for all of God's blessings in general. You might remember that Solomon dedicated the Temple he built, the first Temple, during the Feast of Tabernacles.

How much progress has been made? Have the people kept their commitment to get their priorities right and rebuild the Temple?

Looking again at 2:3, it seems apparent that the Temple rebuilding is now complete. Haggai addresses three questions to the governor, Zerubbabel:

- Who of you is left who saw this house in its former glory?
- How does it look to you now?
- Does it not seem to you like nothing?

That seems kind of harsh, doesn't it? The people have made the right choice, recommitted themselves to their covenant with God, done the hard work, and rebuilt the Temple – now Haggai's going to criticize their results? Sure, it's not as pretty or well done as Solomon's Temple was, but Solomon had a lot more wealth and materials to work with than a group of returned refugees from Babylon!

The questions Haggai asks are rhetorical. What Haggai is doing is asking aloud the questions that are being thought or whispered among the people. Everyone can see that it's not what it was. The glory of this Temple is nothing like Solomon's; this one looks much humbler and simpler. It seems inferior to the Temple that some of them remembered from before its destruction in 587/586 B.C.E.

Those thoughts and whispers could have great power, and Haggai knew he needed to address the "elephant in the room." The people needed encouragement; as Wolfendale says, "murmerers and complainers belong to every age."[7] The people were facing discouragement, and you and I know that it can be easy at times to become discouraged in the work of God.

Why did the results not match the effort? Why was the fruit not as great as we expected? No matter our field of endeavor, we can find discouragement, and doing God's work is no exception. Leaders know this like few others. They see in their mind's eye what could be, and when their efforts don't bring that reality to bear, it's tempting to fall into discouragement and begin asking questions like, "What could I have done differently?" or "Did I completely miss the ball here?"

When we're tempted as individuals, as leaders, or as team members to be discouraged, that's when we need to hear verses four and five of chapter two:

"But now be strong, Zerubbabel,' declares the Lord. 'Be strong, Joshua son of Jozadak, the high priest. Be strong, all you people of the land,' declares the Lord, 'and work. For I am with you,' declares the Lord Almighty. 'This is what I covenanted with you when you came out of Egypt. And my Spirit remains among you. Do not fear.'"

Through the prophet Haggai, God told the leaders (Zerubbabel and Joshua) and the people to be strong. You might remember that a similar command, **"be strong,"** was given to another Joshua, in Joshua 1:8, when he has just assumed the mantle of leadership from Moses to lead the people of Israel and is facing the uncertainty and dangers of the Promised Land. You might remember that same command, **"be strong,"** was given to Solomon by David regarding the building of the first

Temple, in 1 Chronicles 28:20. And now we see it repeated to these leaders in this day.

Leaders, **when you're not sure what's next, and you're tempted by discouragement, look back at what God has said and done in the past.**

Three times here we hear God say, "be strong." When God says something once, we should listen. When He says something twice, we really need to pay close attention. But when He says something three times, we better be listening with our shoes on, ready to do what He says.

God reiterates His promise that He is with His people, just as He said to Moses and Joshua, just as He said to the people through the earlier prophets, just as He said to the people in Haggai's first prophetic sermon. He's not changing His mind; He's not abandoning them; He's not forgetting them. He's faithful to the covenant, just as He promised that He would be in Deuteronomy 12, 14, 16, and 26.

I think what we're seeing here is God speaking not only to fears that may have been whispered, but also to fears that had gone unspoken. I think the people were afraid that God had written an eternal ICHABOD over His people, that all was in vain and that all was lost, that they would never again come to the place of being God's people as they had been in past days. God speaks gently but firmly to that fear. He tells them, **"My Spirit remains among you. Do not fear."** That's the same Spirit that rested on Moses and the elders of Israel as they led the people out of Egypt and through the desert (Numbers 11:25). That's the same Spirit that rested on judges like Samson, who delivered the people from oppression (Judges 14:6). That's the same Spirit that rested on David, who led God's people during the golden era of Israel's history (1 Samuel 16:13).

He tells the people not to fear because He is with them. Is there anything better that we could possibly hear from God?

God told His people through the prophet Haggai that He would be with them. And God has said the same thing to His people today, to you and me and all those who have put their trust and hope in Him. Did you know that? Did you know that if you're a follower of Jesus, that promise applies to you too? Look back at what God has done and see Him at work in your life; He's there!

Notice in verses 6-9 that the name "Lord Almighty" is said FIVE times. I think maybe God's trying to communicate something through His prophet.

Despite a sagging economy - God is still Almighty.

Despite family issues and relationship problems - God is still Almighty.

Despite a pace of life that gets faster and faster and feels as though it will never slow - God is still Almighty.

Remember what God has said. Remember what God has done. Remember that He is Lord Almighty. And be strong and fear not. He is always with His people – then and now.

GOD'S PROMISES

God promises to do three things in verses 6-9:

1. **"I will once more shake the heavens and the earth, the sea and the dry land."** This is the only verse in Haggai that is quoted in the New Testament, in Hebrews 12:26. Robert Alden says, "The first "shaking" took place at Mount Sinai, when God gave the Law to Moses (Exodus 19:6); the second shaking will come at the end of the world. The author of Hebrews then went on to explain that we who are in Christ have an unshakeable kingdom that will survive the earthquake yet to come."[8] God's judgment is coming, and nothing will be left unaffected.

2. **"I will shake all nations."** That's a reaffirmation of the first promise. Repetition is important in Scripture, and here it is expounded on a little more. It won't be just Israel that's shaken; ALL nations will be affected by God's judgment.

3. **"I will fill this house with glory."** Think of the cloud of the Presence that filled the tabernacle that's de-

scribed in Exodus 40:34. Think of the cloud of the Presence that filled the Temple when Solomon dedicated it, described in 2 Chronicles 5:14. Those were nothing compared to what is coming. When Jesus comes to this Temple, God's presence will be evident as never before.

Promises one and two are about God's judgment. Promise three is about God's grace.

God tells the people: **"The silver is mine and the gold is mine."** Here we see God telling the people that all the materials that they were so envious of that made Solomon's Temple the amazing sight that it was all belonged to Him. And they still do. Despite the lack of "grandeur" that the people remembered from the previous Temple, this Temple would be honored beyond their ability to comprehend, because the Messiah would come to this Temple. He would climb its steps; He would pray in its courtyard; He would sacrifice and worship within its gates. **"The glory of this house will be greater than that of the former house"** because Messiah will walk in this one.

The materal possessions and financial resources of the nations that they prize so much will eventually be brought to build the temple. We know from Nehemiah that the Persians would underwrite the construction costs in the 5th century B.C.E., fulfilling this prophecy. All things, including these valuables, ultimately belong to the sovereign Lord, and they are His to use as He sees fit.

"The desired of all nations will come." Among all people in all nations there is an aching and a craving of the human heart, longing for restoration from its decay. We know that this sinful fallen world is not how it's supposed to be, and we long to see healing come. That desire of all nations will come, and we will see ultimate fulfillment of this through the Messiah's work in restoring our relationship with God and reversing the curse of Eden.

"And in this place I will grant peace." Peace is more than just the absence of conflict and strife; the Hebrew word "shalom" speaks of completeness, wholeness, and integrity in every sense. It's a picture of wellness and soundness in a holistic way, in every part of life.

Haggai has taught us much so far. Three truths that stand out to me from chapter two are:

1. God always delivers on His promises.
2. Everything is God's.
3. God can and will grant real peace.

Leaders, Haggai taught the people a principle that we would do well to take to heart: **It's all God's – our time, our talents and skills, our financial resources – to use as He desires.**

So far in Haggai, we've spent some time in self-examination and in evaluating our current situation and circumstances in light of our obedience to God's Word. Let's continue processing the truths of this book together.

As I look at what is in my hand (my time, my talents, my resources), am I more concerned with using them as God would desire or as I would desire?

What is the next step in my plan to grow in this area? To be intentional, plan with the end in mind, but plan some steps or benchmarks between you and your goal.

What steps am I going to take this week to grow in my obedience to what God is asking of me with regard to my stewardship, not just of money, but of all of my life?

God promises that He will grant real peace. What area of your life would you ask Him to grant peace in right now?

FINAL WORDS

The book of Haggai closes with his third message or sermon presented in two parts. For the final time, we see God's instruction to the people through His prophet to evaluate their priorities. This message was given on the twenty-fourth day of the ninth month; that's December 18 on our calendar, the time when winter crops would have been planted. The question must have arisen among the people: "Will this year be any different from the last years of famine, drought, and pestilence?"

Haggai then directs a question to the priests. One of the major duties of the priests was to provide Torah instruction for the people, and they were subject to indictment when they did not. Haggai had two questions for the priests: Is holiness contagious? Is sin contagious?

If I take my hand and dip it in blue paint and then place my palm on a white sheet of paper, I'll leave a blue handprint, right? What about if I take a clean hand and place my palm on a white sheet of paper – will I leave a clean mark?

Haggai teaches the priests, the teachers of the law, a lesson from God regarding holiness. For something to be holy means that it's acceptable to God; it's something set apart for a specific task or purpose. Alternately, for something to be defiled means that it's unacceptable to God. Haggai's object lesson to the priests is that defilement is transmitted much more easily than holiness.

Defilement is catching, contagious; holiness is not.

It is easier to fall into sin than to fall into righteousness. Defilement can come by the company we keep. Psalm 1:1-3 says,

"Blessed is the one who does not walk in step with the wicked or stand in the way that sinners take or sit in the company of mockers, but whose delight is in the law of the Lord, and who meditates on his law day and night. That person is like a tree planted by streams of water, which yields its fruit in season and whose leaf does not wither whatever they do prospers."

And 1 Corinthians 15:33 says, **"Do not be misled: "Bad company corrupts good character."** Association with the wrong crowd will have bad effects on us, just as the Psalmist contrasts the way of the wicked with the way of the righteous. Holiness, though, comes only through direct contact with God. It's been well said that "God has no grandchildren."

Haggai's lesson on holiness and purity reminds us that the sin of disobedience makes our actions and our worship unacceptable to God (defiled).

We distinguish between the secular and the religious, but that's not a biblical distinction. All parts of our lives must come under God's Lordship and leadership. That's why we are told in Leviticus 19:2 and by Jesus Himself to **"be holy, as the Lord your God is holy."**

Haggai challenges the idea of a purely secular society with the truths that everything is God's, and everything needs to be done under His leadership. If people are not right with God, their society will reflect their character, not change it.

The people had sinned, and that sin made their worship and their offerings unacceptable to God. As human beings, our acts of sacrifice and worship are defiled by the touch of our fallen hands. Only through Jesus, the One who transforms our fallenness through His death and resurrection, can our sacrifices be acceptable before God. Mark Boda reminds us that Haggai 2:10-14 is a humbling reminder of our fallenness and a vivid depiction of the insidious nature of sin that threatens our relationship with God.[9]

Just restoring and rebuilding the temple is not enough; there must be changes in the lives of the people, in their priorities and in their hearts. When our attitudes are wrong, nothing given to God is acceptable because what we offer is defiled. God wants hearts, not hands; He wants obedience, not sacrifice (Hosea 6:6).

In verses 15-18, we see God say not once or twice, but three times: "give careful thought." Sounds a whole lot like what we started with – "consider your ways" – doesn't it? But we see something else repeated three times too – "from this day on." Three times, God tells them to give careful thought, and three times He tells them what will happen "from this day on." We see the tension as the people remember where they are. They remember the disobedience they had fallen into. They remember the apathy and discouragement.

Remembering our sins of the past helps to keep us from making those mistakes again. Over and over we are told to remember the past and remember what God has done. Why do we remember our past sins so well? God has forgotten them - why can't we? Remembering our sins helps us to remember how much we are truly in need of God's grace, mercy, and forgiveness.

And then God says in verse 19, **"from this day on I will bless you."** In other words, "Because of your renewed devotion and obedience, I will bless you. Because you chose to come home to Me, I will bless you." Can you imagine the shouts of joy among the people? Can you see them grinning ear to ear, from the oldest to the youngest, as they understood what Haggai was saying to them? Can you imagine how they felt on that day?

Each person is responsible to God for their own relationship with Him, and holiness comes through direct contact only. The most important reminders for the people of God are to love Him with all their hearts, souls, minds, and strength, and to do what He says.

Haggai closes this message with the news that God will bless them. An exciting time was about to begin because of their obedience and renewed devotion.

Process through these questions with me:

"God wants our hearts, not our hands only." Does God have your heart? Are you wholly and completely devoted to Him? In what areas of your life are you holding back?

We don't like to remember times when we've failed and sinned, but remembering can be a help in preventing our walking down those roads again. Spend some time thinking about roads you've been down that were not pleasing to God. Do those memories serve as deterrents for you not to sin again? Commit your ways to God; read and meditate on Psalm 1.

Do you have a personal relationship with God? Are you growing in your spiritual journey?

What attitudes or actions are hindering your worship?

FINAL WORDS, PART 2

Have you ever watched a football game where the intensity just got hotter and hotter? Unfortunately, my favorite team the Dallas Cowboys haven't been in any Super Bowls as of late, but there have been quite a few nail biting game endings in recent years. It seems that the game builds, and builds, and builds, until the final 5 minutes of the fourth quarter when it's just white hot. Fans are on the edges of their seats, and some even go so far as to yell at the television (I don't know anything about that…)

Haggai so far has been like that, building slowly but surely, and as we close this chapter, we'll look at the final words of this prophet that are recorded for us in Scripture.

Remember, this is part two of the sermon that Haggai gave earlier that same day. This one is directed to Zerubbabel, the governor of Judah. It's the shortest of the four messages, and the only one addressed to a single person.

God repeats that He will shake the heavens and the earth, and again we are reminded of the Exodus and Mount Sinai, just like in 2:6. God will overturn and overthrow, alluding to the story in Genesis 19:25 of Sodom and Gomorrah. The reference to chariots, horses, and riders refers to the Exodus, when Pharaoh's army was destroyed in the Red Sea (Exodus 15).

The final verse in this book begins **"On that Day."** When that phrase is used by the prophets, it almost invariably refers to the "Day of the Lord" (Isaiah 2; Joel 1:15, Zechariah 2:11). The Day of the Lord was a way of referring to the day when God would set things right, when goodness and righteousness would prevail. The people of Israel looked forward to that day as a time of vindication and exaltation as the people of God, but the prophets often told the people they shouldn't be so eager, for it was also to be a day of judgment, and they weren't ready for it. It was a reference to the day when God would come in all His glory and sin would be destroyed, when life would be as God in the beginning intended it to be.

In this closing, we see four statements addressed to Zerubbabel:

1) **"I will take you."** The idea is to take possession of something. This is frequently used of God's choice of someone for a special mission (e.g. Abraham, Israel, the Levites, David, Amos). The word denotes a new relationship and the receiving of a new mission in life

2) **"My servant."** A title of honor used elsewhere in the Old Testament of prophets and leaders like Abraham, Moses, Joshua, and David. This was Isaiah's favorite description of the Messiah.

3) **"I will make you a signet ring."** This is a reversal of the curse that Jeremiah had pronounced on Jehoiachin and his descendants. Jehoiachin was the last king of Judah who surrendered Jerusalem to Nebuchadnezzar of Babylon in 597 B.C.E. (Jeremiah 22:24-30). The ancient rabbis taught that Jehoiachin later repented to God and He reversed His sentence. The signet ring was a symbol of authority given to the earthly representative of a heavenly King.

4) **"I have chosen you."** This is intentional divine selection with a specific function in mind. We see it also in Isaiah 41:8-9 and 42:1.

That's all well and good for Zerubbabel, but what does that mean for you and me?

Through Jesus the Messiah, we too are God's possession, taken by Him as His possession for a special mission in life that He has given to us.

Through Jesus the Messiah, we too are God's servants. We live lives in submission to our God, seeking as His disciples to please Him.

Through Jesus the Messiah, we too are God's representatives. We are God's representatives on earth, His hands and feet, and we speak His truth and His offer of hope and purpose to a world that lacks both. As His representatives and bearers of the hope of the world, we have been given the authority of Christ to make disciples of all nations.

Through Jesus the Messiah, we too are God's chosen ones. God has chosen you and me; He has extended a hand to every person who lives and invited him or her into a relationship with Him. Just like Zerubbabel, we have not earned this, and we don't deserve it; that's why it's called grace.

There is a HUGE message of hope here at the end of Haggai, a glowing promise of the Messiah that brings encouragement and new hope to the people of Israel as well as to you and me.

As we close Haggai, I have two questions for you. Have you accepted what God offers – hope, a purpose, and a new life with Him? And if you have, are you living according to the mission and purpose that He has for you?

Let's close this chapter by processing through these questions:

On a scale of 1 to 10, how true is the following statement in your life? Because I am God's possession,

He directs my life and provides leadership and a new mission in life for me.

How is my life reflective of being a servant of God? In what ways is it not?

How can I be God's representative in my circles of influence?

What does it mean to be chosen by God? How does this affect my life, my family, my decision-making processes, my career, and my stewardship of time and money that God has given to me?

We have the authority of Christ to do what He said - make disciples of all nations. How am I involved in doing that? How can I get involved in doing that?

PRINCIPLES FROM HAGGAI

- Give careful thought to your ways.
- A proper perspective is pivotal.

- When you're not sure what's next, and you're tempted by discouragement, look back at what God has said and done in the past.
- It's all God's – our time, our talents and skills, our financial resources – to use as He desires.

6 HABAKKUK

"Habakkuk is above all else a book about the purposes of God and about the realization of His will for His world... it is primarily concerned with how God is keeping His promises to His chosen people Israel, and through them, to humankind."

-- Elizabeth Achtemeier

Political fear and uncertainty. Economic disaster looming large. Anxiety and nervousness about the future running rampant. This sounds kind of familiar, doesn't it? These could have been among the leading headlines in Jerusalem in the years between 609 and 606 B.C.E., and it was to this world that the prophet Habakkuk spoke.

Habakkuk is a small, often overlooked book in the Old Testament that has a significant message for the people of his day and for ours if we will only take the time to listen and understand. Habakkuk asked questions that the people of his day were asking in the midst of their anxiety and suffering – questions like, how can the wicked prosper? How can God not answer when the righteous suffer? Habakkuk was not content simply to hear human philosophies or opinions about these questions. He asked God to answer these questions, much as Jeremiah, Moses, Job, and the Psalmist had done before him.

We tend to think of prophets as those who foretold the future when in fact, the vast majority of Old Testament prophecy is forth telling, not foretelling. The prophets were covenant enforcers; they reminded the people of what God had said and done in the past, most often referencing what we know today as the book of Deuteronomy, and they were straightforward in their presentation of truth. No white washing, no meandering about the truth; most of the time, their prophecy was simple, unvarnished truth about the people's actions and hearts.

God would send his prophets to the people to remind them about His hopes and desires for them. We read in Genesis 12 that God's dream for His people is that they would be blessed <u>so that</u> they would be a blessing to the whole world, so that everyone would be blessed through them. And in the pages of the Old Testament, we read that the people of God turned away from that, instead focusing on themselves and their wants and desires. God sent the prophets into that situation to speak truth into the people's lives. He wanted the people to know that He still had a plan and He wanted them to choose His way, not their own.

Habakkuk's message is set against a backdrop of real people facing real questions about real human suffering. Anyone who experiences terrible difficulty in life will benefit from studying this book. God tells Habakkuk that His people will experience the end of prosperity, the end of their political autonomy, the increased success of the wicked, and the withdrawal of God's protection because of their spiritual apathy toward and disobedience of God.

We have no family statement about Habakkuk: no father's name, no hometown, no indication of what tribe he belonged to. We know less about him than just about any other prophet. We don't know how old he was, whether or not he was married or had children, or what his occupation was.

We know from this text two primary things: he prayed courageously to God and he was a prophet. The meaning of Habakkuk's name is somewhat disputed. It comes either from the Assyrian language and refers to a type of garden plant or from a Hebrew root word that means, "to embrace."

The events described in Habakkuk took place approximately between 609 and 606 B.C.E. Habakkuk lived at the same time as three other Old Testament prophets: Jeremiah, Nahum, and Zephaniah. This book is unique among the prophets in that it is Habakkuk who initiated the conversation with God. In the case of the other prophets, it is said that "the word of the Lord came to" or "through" the prophet, but here, Habakkuk initiated the discussion.

Habakkuk was an honest believer with honest doubts who searched for truth at its source: God Himself.

WHAT HABAKKUK SAID

I think a better translation here for **"the prophecy that Habakkuk the prophet received"** would be "the <u>burden</u> that Habakkuk the prophet received." What we will soon discover is that this man of God has been praying with all his heart and strength for God to intervene in the world around him, and his prayers have seemingly affected nothing. He is burdened by what he sees, but it is nothing compared to the burden that he will soon receive when God answers him.

God burdening? Can we see God doing that? I think so. Habakkuk is questioning God, seeking an answer. He is struggling to understand the ways of God. The answer will burden Habakkuk even more than he already is, but he comes earnestly seeking and listening, and God responds. The answer will not be what Habakkuk wanted or hoped for; it is a message of heavy judgment, thus the burden. But he does receive an answer. And that answer will resonate with all those who share Habakkuk's doubts, fears, and frustrations.

"How long, Lord, must I call for help, but you do not listen?" This phrasing is very reminiscent of the psalms; in fact, Habakkuk's words indicate a knowledge of the psalms that is significant. Based on his knowledge of the psalms, as well as from the song he writes that is chapter 3 in his prophetic book, some theologians have even suggested that Habakkuk was a Levitical priest who served on staff at the Temple. Habakkuk's words are in the form of a lament psalm; that's a type of psalm characterized by crying out to God, of searching for answers to the "why" questions that plague all of us at times in this life. Check out Psalm 13 and Psalm 22 for examples of lament psalms. Why does evil seem to go unpunished? Why does God not respond to prayer?

Palmer Robertson has written that Habakkuk's phrase "how long" seems to indicate that Habakkuk had spent quite some time in prayer already about these issues.[1] This was not the first time he had brought this to God. He's been persistent with this, over and over presenting his arguments and his requests to God. And now in verse two, it seems he has come to a point of confusion and doubt, of being utterly puzzled over the silence of God. He simply cannot understand how God can allow the situation to continue any longer.

Habakkuk feels as though God is ignoring him. He is screaming to God for help; he is pointing out injustice to a holy God, and the heavens are silent.

In reading about Habakkuk's anguish and pain over God's silence, I'm reminded of a story that John Ortberg tells in his outstanding book *Know Doubt* about a couple he had known for a long time who had a beautiful daughter. He says, "She was the kind of child who was so beautiful that people would stop them on the street to comment on her beauty. They were the kind of parents you would hope every child might have.

They had a pool in their backyard.

One summer day, it was so nice outside that the mom set up the playpen in the backyard so that her daughter could enjoy the day. The phone rang, and her daughter was in the playpen, so she went in to answer the phone. Her daughter tugged on the wall of that playpen, and the hinge that held the side up gave way. It didn't have to. God could have stopped it. God could have reached down from heaven and straightened it out and kept that playpen up. He didn't. The hinge gave way, and the side came down, and the baby crawled out, and heaven was silent.

When that mom came outside, she saw the beautiful little body of her beloved daughter at the bottom of that pool. It was the beginning of a pain that no words could name."[2]

The heavens were silent as that mom screamed out to God to fix this, to correct the injustice that she saw in what happened. And Habakkuk feels a similar way: that he has been crying out and screaming to a holy and just God to correct the injustice and violence that he sees all around him. And he has heard nothing. So in verse 2, he cries out again – **"how long, O Lord, must I call for help, but you do not listen? Or cry out to you "violence!" but you do not save?"**

You can see this question posed throughout the Scriptures, from Job to the disciples of Jesus. In Mark 4:35, the disciples were in a boat and a storm was in full swing. They were afraid for their lives, and Jesus was asleep on the boat. They woke him and asked Him, "Don't you care if we drown?"

Leaders can learn from this: **Our questions can reveal our perspective.**

Leaders know to ask questions, but asking the right questions is crucial. Our questions can many times reveal what our perspective is.

This is true in Habakkuk's case. Habakkuk struggles with unanswered prayer. "You do not save" – that is, You don't deliver Your people from what is oppressing them. He struggles because he's not sure that God cares. His question reveals his perspective.

What Habakkuk is asking here is in essence – "God, if You are good and holy and just, and if You are all powerful and all knowing and ever present, how can You allow what happens on this planet to happen? How can You allow a child to die, people to starve, wars to happen again and again, and conflict to occur everywhere? Why don't You just fix it all? Why do You tolerate the sin that is all around us when You can fix it all?" Do you hear the accusation here: "You tolerate." You can do something about this, God! Why don't You?

These questions were applicable in Habakkuk's day. The people of Judah were facing destruction. With every day, their future grew dimmer and dimmer. The Babylonian Empire was on the rise, and the people of Judah knew that their days as an independent power were numbered. They did not have the ability to resist Babylon, and their political freedom, their economic future, and even their lives were all in imminent jeopardy. And so the righteous among the people of God were asking "I thought we were the people of God. Where is He when we need Him?" Everything they stood for and everything their nation was founded on was slowly being eroded. Where was God?

Habakkuk knows from Scripture that God is holy, righteous, and good. As is said in Exodus 34, God is

"compassionate and gracious, slow to anger, abounding in love and faithfulness, maintaining love to thousands, and forgiving wickedness, re bellion, and sin. Yet he does not leave the guilty unpunished."

Habakkuk understands this; but how then can God leave the guilty unpunished in Habakkuk's day? Where is God now?

Habakkuk's lament continues, **"therefore the law is paralyzed, and justice never prevails. The wicked hem in the righteous, so that justice is perverted."**

Habakkuk's prayer here reveals not only that they were facing problems from outside their country, but also that the very fabric of their own society was coming apart at the seams. Many people in the nation of Judah were no longer following the ways of God. Spiritual apostasy was rampant; as in the days of the judges, people did what was right in their own eyes, not following the law of God, but, instead, doing whatever they wanted. They had fallen away from the standards laid out in the covenant that God had made with His people at Sinai. They were acting wickedly, and it seemed that justice never prevailed. The wicked became more and more powerful, and the righteous were oppressed by violence and injustice. Justice was perverted because the courts were corrupted by bribery. God's Law, which should have guaranteed justice in society, was being ignored and mocked by the people's disobedience and corruption. What could they do?

Habakkuk cries out to God. He is surrounded by injustice and violence, the wicked are prospering and the righteous are not, and it seems as though the law is paralyzed. Where is God when they need Him? Habakkuk has begun to doubt; judgment is delayed, so can God truly be just and good? He does not seem to be afraid to bring his doubts, his fears, and his anguish to God. His understanding of God as just and righteous and holy is not lining up with his current experience of God.

Has that ever been your experience as well? Have you ever brought similar complaints to God concerning His apparent silence and absence?

And so ends Habakkuk's opening prayer. He is in anguish over what he sees around him. He is astounded and dismayed that God has not stepped in and intervened on behalf of His people.

I believe that Habakkuk came to God in this book with five questions:

    a. God, do You care?

    b. Do You see what's happening?

    c. How long will You continue to allow this?

    d. Are You good?

    e. Are You just?

These are not small questions, and to our ears, they might sound a bit arrogant. Habakkuk, are you seriously asking God if He is good – if He is just – if He cares?

And yet God does not condemn this honest, searching heart; in fact, God rewards it in His decision to answer Habakkuk's questions. Habakkuk refuses to ignore his doubts; he wants an answer and he honestly seeks after truth, even when it is painful.

What do we do when God doesn't make sense? How do we respond when God's actions don't seem to line up with who we believe Him to be?

Through the words of Scripture, we can gain perspective. We can gain a better understanding of who God is. We can see His words and actions through a large part of human history, and by reading and studying His Word, we can learn about God and His character and His nature. Our knowledge is incomplete to be sure, but He has given us His Word as a tool to help us grow in our knowledge and understanding of Him and His love for us.

I was talking with a friend of mine a few years ago about Habakkuk's questions, and he noted that it's important to remember that our questions can reveal our thought processes. The question that Habakkuk asks and the question that the disciples ask on the boat seems to indicate a belief that God wants us never to experience distress or discomfort, a belief that if God really loved us, He would make everything comfortable and easy and stable.

As I look at Scripture, as I learn from men and women of faith who have gone before us throughout history, and as I reflect on my own personal experience, I see though that distress and discomfort are often the most fertile of soils for our growth. Many, many times, we don't look for God without them. Sometimes, we don't even THINK about God without them. We just enjoy our stress free lives and figure that we're doing ok and being stress free is our reward.

But when stress or hardship or difficulty occurs in our lives that exceeds our ability to navigate or control it, we talk to God seemingly endlessly, pleading with him to do something, much as Habakkuk does here.

My friend pointed out the similarity with the book of Job as well. Even the way the book of Job is written at the beginning pulls us toward the mindset that when things begin going badly with Job, he is being forsaken unjustly, so our whole presupposition is that Job doesn't deserve any of this hardship because he hasn't done anything to warrant it. He has been faithful to God and to his family. Why should he suffer? Isn't this unjust? The bottom line question we ask is: **What did he do to deserve this?**

But the question that we never ask in the beginning of the book, when Job is so richly blessed and so abundantly wealthy, is: **What did he do to deserve that?**

The answer to both questions is the same...nothing.

God's desire is to bless us and love us, not to discipline us unfairly or capriciously. But our perspective can seem to indicate otherwise, much the way a child can interpret discipline as cruel instead of loving. Our perspective is often focused around "what's good for me?" And since that's all that God should be interested in, God should always do that which is most pleasurable to me, right?

In reality, God loves us too much to do that. Just as we love our children too much to allow them to do things that can cause long-term pain or hardship, God loves us too much to allow us to stay "me-focused." As we mature as Christ-followers, we begin to shift our focus from being "me-centered" to being "God-centered."

It is our expectation of God's "job description" that fails in our eyes, not God Himself. Habakkuk had questions (and we do too) because our understanding of what God should and will do is based more on our expectations than His actual character as revealed in Scripture. We have to ask ourselves, "Is my faith based more on my expectations of God or on what His Word says about Him?" He is just and He will call the wicked to account, but it is in His time, not ours. I like how Pastor Waylon Bailey says it: "Salvation is not prosperity now. Salvation is trust in the midst of hardship while God plans His actions according to His ultimate knowledge and will."

In fact, the hardship and difficulty about which Habakkuk is lamenting built a group of men like Habakkuk, Jeremiah, and Nahum who desperately longed for Him and endlessly sought His will and wisdom. Isn't that what God ultimately wants?

We have to remember, in times like those faced by Habakkuk as well as the times we face today, that God is loving and sovereign. He is still on His throne. In His great love, He has permitted mankind to choose their way; that's the doctrine of free will: that we can choose to follow Him or choose not to and go our own way. Free will has consequences; if we choose poorly, those choices are like dominoes that affect so many other things and other people. When we choose to disobey God and go our own way, the consequences will only add to the sin level of our world. To the surprise of no one, we live in a fallen world; evil seems to be rampant and unchecked at times, and people choose to participate in unspeakable horrors. One has only to look back at the twentieth century to see examples of how evil people can be when they choose their own way instead of God's, and the start of

the twenty-first century has not promised any improve-
ment.

Yet despite what we see, hear, and experience, we believe what Scripture teaches us: that God is not on vaca-
tion. He is still on His throne; He is sovereign over all. He
has chosen to allow us to live in the midst of this sinful,
fallen world that is such because of our choices. It is not
as He created it, and Paul tells us that all of creation is
crying out for the re-creation of all things that will come
in the end (Romans 8:19-22). What was in the days of
Habakkuk – what is in ours – is not the way things will
always be.

Jesus taught his disciples to pray that what is true in
heaven would be true on earth as well – that we would
pray that "up there" would come "down here." Part of
our mission as Christ followers is to live in such a way
that reflects that prayer – that we would respond to others with love, not hate; with peace, not violence; with
generosity, not greed; with inclusion, not exclusion; and
with community, not isolation. When we look at the fall-
en world around us, we have to take some responsibility

for it. We have to commit ourselves and what God has entrusted to us to God's Kingdom, so that God's will will be done on earth as it is in Heaven.

We live in a time of uncertainty. If you look at our current political landscape, our economic system that seems at times very unstable, and our world that is in turmoil, it is hard to deny the times of turmoil in this life. But one thing I know to be sure; there is one foundation stone that has not and will not move. There is one truth that will outlast every political party, every economic system, every nation, every constitution, and every politician: God is loving and sovereign. It is on that truth that I build my life and my perspective. Despite what happens around me, despite the condition of my flocks and my herds, despite the condition of my 401K, despite the angry, vitriolic, mudslinging that I have witnessed in our public arena, God is still loving and sovereign, and His purposes will not be deterred in the slightest.

As Christ-followers, we might know this in our heads, but I'm hearing from Habakkuk that it's important that we allow it to migrate to our hearts. God is loving and He is sovereign over all, despite our perceptions at times to the contrary. We have to understand that He knows more than we do; He has a different perspective than we do; and we must trust in Him. Our trust is not found in chariots; our trust is not found in politicians, political party platforms, governments, military might, our 401Ks or our bank accounts. Our trust is to be found solely in the Lord our God, because He is loving and sovereign.

That's my second leadership principle from Habakkuk: **God is loving and sovereign, and we find our trust and hope solely in Him.** I think we need to remember this, to hide this truth in our hearts and allow God's Word to refocus our perspective so that we do not put our faith or trust in ANYONE or ANYTHING other than God. God can be trusted all the time, in any crisis, in any circumstance.

Habakkuk has asked his questions – now what?

Will God respond?

WHAT GOD SAID

He does. God begins speaking in verse 5, responding to what Habakkuk has said.

"Look at the nations and watch—and be utterly amazed. For I am going to do something in your days that you would not believe, even if you were told."

But notice what God does not say. He does not say that He's glad Habakkuk brought this to His attention; He does not say that He's been out of town or asleep and hasn't noticed what's going on. Instead, God begins by encouraging Habakkuk to look beyond the borders of his own nation and to be amazed because He is at work.

In Habakkuk's day, the common thought was that gods were localized. That is, the gods of the Babylonians held no authority over or impact on the Assyrian people or the Egyptians. You might think of the popular perception of the day like this: gods had borders, much like nations or kings. Inside those borders, they were in charge, but not outside. God tells Habakkuk that He is currently, actively at work in the world, and that Habakkuk can see that if he looks beyond his own borders.

I think we're no different in many ways. We are very concerned to see God doing what we think He should do in our country and in our backyards, and we wonder, if He doesn't fulfill our expectations, if He is actively involved in the world at all today. But if we look with Habakkuk beyond our borders, we can see the hand of God moving in the world, moving the course of history toward the ultimate conclusion that He has promised through His Word.

Habakkuk is told to look around and watch. What is about to happen will amaze you; it is something that is unbelievable. The words for "look" and "watch" here are the same words that Habakkuk had used in his prayer to God when he asked, "Why do you make me <u>look</u> at injustice?" "Why do you tolerate, or <u>watch</u>, wrong?"

God continues: **"I am raising up the Babylonians, that ruthless and impetuous people, who sweep**

across the whole earth to seize dwellings not their own."

God says that He is raising up the Babylonians to judge the people of Judah.

Wait a minute – what???

Habakkuk has to be rocked back on his heels with that first statement. You're doing WHAT?

Have you ever been rocked back like that from something that God said in His Word or did in your life? I have, and it's rarely expected. Yet in those times, I've often gained a new appreciation for and understanding of who God is and what He is doing.

The Babylonians, also called the Chaldeans or the neo-Babylonians, came to power under the leadership of a man named Nabopolassar in 625 B.C.E. They reached the pinnacle of their empire under king Nebuchadnezzar between 605 and 562 B.C.E. It is as they were rising to the height of their power that God revealed these words to Habakkuk: "I am raising up the Babylonians."

How can this be? A holy God, using a people like the Babylonians to execute judgment on His chosen people?

Babylon was known for its military prowess and success. **"They sweep across the whole earth,"** and no one can stop them. Not the Egyptians, not the Assyrians, and surely not the tiny nation of Judah. They are a **"feared and dreaded people"** indeed. No one wanted to be standing in the way of the Babylonian army when it came marching through. They practiced a true scorched earth policy of warfare, leaving only destruction and death in their wake. They were irresistible as a military force. Page Kelley describes them as a nation who worshipped at the altar of their military might. [3]

God told Habakkuk that the Babylonians were a law to themselves and promoted their own honor; they were arrogant enough to believe that they answered to no one. They were above any law and they prided themselves in their self-sufficiency. Do you see the picture that God is painting here for Habakkuk? It's not pretty.

Habakkuk's prayer to God had been focused around the issue of how God could allow His people to behave wickedly and violently, seemingly without repercussion. God answered Habakkuk that the repercussions were coming, and they were going to be violent indeed.

"Their hordes advance like a desert wind and gather prisoners like sand." Throughout the Old Testament, sand had been used as a symbol of the blessing and promise of God to His people. Your descendants "will be as numerous as the sand" Abraham was told; and yet here, the symbol is turned upside down. Here, sand is used in the context of national defeat and shame.

"They deride kings and scoff at rulers. They laugh at all fortified cities; they build earthen ramps and capture them. Then they sweep past like the wind and go on – guilty men, whose own strength is their god."

The Babylonians believed they could not be defeated. No one stood in their path! They could conquer any enemy, defeat any foe, and then move on to the next. The last line is quite telling: "guilty men, whose own strength is their god." They have turned their military might and strength into an idol. They believed that they had built themselves into what they were and that they were responsible for all that they had. They owed no allegiance to anyone or anything, including God. Or so they believed.

But think back to verse 6 – God says, **"I am raising up the Babylonians."**

Despite what the Babylonians themselves thought about it, God allowed their rise to power. He was directing this orchestra for His purposes. And here, what was vague becomes clear. God used this evil, wicked, violent people to judge His people in Judah because His people had turned away from Him.

Habakkuk asked in the first part of this chapter "Why do You tolerate wrong?" Will the wicked never be punished?

God answered, "Yes they will. Punishment is coming."

God is holy and just and loving. And just as parents will not allow their children to act in ways that harm them, God will get the attention of His people. He desires that they remember the source of all things: Him. Everything that they have, everything that they are, comes from Him and Him alone.

He had sent prophet after prophet to Judah to get the people's attention, to call them back to the ways of God, but time after time they rejected the message of the prophets. Their attitude was, "We'll live life the way we want to, thank you very much. We'll cry out to You when things are tough, God, but unless we're in dire straights, please leave us alone. We'll come to You when it's convenient for us. We'll holler when we need something, ok?"

That's not the way it works.

Judgment is due, and judgment is coming. But it is surely not how Habakkuk hoped or prayed for it to come.

The Babylonians would not distinguish between the righteous or wicked in Judah. They would simply come, destroying and looting and killing indiscriminately. We like to think that our actions and choices affect only us; in fact, Scripture teaches that sin has consequences for the community as well as the individual. That's the case here in Judah.

I think Habakkuk had a preferred solution in mind when he prayed in the first verses of this chapter. And I think that what God described was <u>not</u> it.

What can we see here? What can we learn from this passage of Scripture? A few things I think.

First, we see that **God is at work**. Despite our perceptions or appearances to the contrary, God is at work in this world. His plan will come to pass; no one can stop it or hinder it. He is never surprised, never shocked, never having to go to plan B. That is comforting and encouraging to us as His people because many times things don't go as we expect them to go. Our plans go awry, our world seems to spin out of control, and we are left to wonder if God stepped away from the controls for a moment. God's words to Habakkuk speak clearly to this; He is always at work, even when we think He's not.

Second, I think we see that **God's Word is eternal.** Events will happen just as He said they would. In Deuteronomy 28:49 and following, God had warned the people of Israel eight hundred years before the time of Habakkuk that if they turned away from Him, He would send an enemy nation to judge them. Again and again, God had sent his prophets to warn the people of the evil of turning away from Him, and the people had refused to listen. And now we see God declaring that what He had said so long ago would indeed come to pass. A covenant with God is serious business. We must take God's Word, His revealed truth, seriously. He will do what He said He will do. His charge to us as His people is to live lives that are worthy of the calling that we have received, to be His people in the midst of a fallen world, and to share the hope that we have received with others so that they too can find abundant life both now and forever. This is not optional, not an activity for when we retire or for when we have time; it's for today, now.

Third, we see that **God judges as guilty those whose strength is their god**. In today's world, we honor the strong, the ones who are self-made men and women who rely on no one else. God's Word, though, sees the folly of looking at your strength, the work of your hands, as your god. We may not bow down to it, and we may not make idols of wood or clay anymore, but there are assuredly idols in our modern world. We idolize our strength as individuals and as a nation. We are self-reliant people whose strength is our god. Can it be said that a Christ follower, a disciple of Jesus, sees his or her strength as worthy of praise or honor? The Babylonians promoted their own honor – that is, they tooted their own horn. They made sure that everyone knew about their accomplishments so that they could be revered and honored and respected and feared. Those who follow God, though, choose a different path. As the Psalmist said so well in Psalm 20:7, **"some trust in chariots and some in horses, but we trust in the name of the Lord our God."** Our strength is not our God; God alone is worthy of our trust and praise and honor, never ourselves and never our own strength. In verse 11, God calls those who saw their strength as their god "guilty" in His eyes – and the same is true today.

Habakkuk thought God was not active enough. He thought God didn't care about the injustice and violence and wickedness in the world. But God revealed that He was indeed active – just not the way Habakkuk expected.

In 1 Peter 3:8-9, Peter writes these words,

"But do not forget this one thing, dear friends: with the Lord a day is like a thousand years, and a thousand years are like a day. The Lord is not slow in keeping his promise, as some understand slowness. He is patient with you, not wanting anyone to perish, but everyone to come to repentance."

God had been very patient with the people of Judah. He had sent prophets to remind them of His Word; He had shown them in many mighty ways His great love for them, and He had in the past given them righteous rulers to lead them in the ways of God. But ultimately, the people chose to turn away from God. They chose to reject Him and His ways. They rejected His authority, and God allowed them to do so because He had given them the gift of free will.

But even in the midst of a message of judgment like this, if we look, we can see what John Ortberg calls "grace notes" in the background of this musical score. Even this judgment by the Babylonians should be seen in light of God's love. Proverbs 3:12 says that the Lord disciplines those whom He loves. He loves His people, and here that love is reflected in that they will face the consequences of their actions and attitudes. But God is not finished with His people. Judgment is not the final word here; more is still to come.

I think leaders need to note here Habakkuk's point that **sin is never overlooked by God; it must be dealt**

with. But remember that God is a God of love as well as of justice. He is both, one neither more nor less than the other. Grace was extended to His people in Habakkuk's time, just as it is today. No matter where we've been, no matter what we've done, God extends His grace and love to every one of us who earnestly seeks Him and calls out to Him. Every person who comes to Him will be wrapped in His embrace, and every person who truly turns from their sin will be forgiven and given the gift of abundant life, both now and forever. Judgment is hard, but God is still in charge, and He wants His people ultimately to come home to Him.

HABAKKUK'S RESPONSE

Habakkuk hears what God says, and he responds from his heart, beginning to expound on attributes of God.

"O Lord, are you not from everlasting? My God, my Holy One, we will not die." What surprised Habakkuk about God's response was not that judgment was coming; he had prayed for that very thing! What surprised him was the agent of God's judgment – the nation of Babylon. Habakkuk doesn't understand how God, Who is holy and just, can use the wicked and profane nation of Babylon to judge His chosen people in Judah.

Here, Habakkuk speaks of God as being **"from everlasting"** – that is, that He has always been and will always be. God's existence is never in question; he will never cease to be. Habakkuk then says because of that truth that His people, those that He has called to Himself to be His own, will not cease to be either. They cannot be annihilated by Babylon because then how would God's promises to Abraham, Isaac, and Jacob be fulfilled? Habakkuk believes that God's people will never be totally destroyed.

Habakkuk calls God **"my God, my Holy One"**, focusing on his personal relationship with God. This is not impersonal at all; this is very personal.

"O Lord, you have appointed them to execute judgment; O Rock, you have ordained them to punish." God has "appointed" and "ordained" the Babylonians to execute judgment; that is, they've been set aside for this purpose. And in the midst of this declaration of truth, Habakkuk calls God "Rock" – a source of security and protection, immovable. We see this term used for God throughout the Psalms. God – our rock, our fortress, our protector.

"Your eyes are too pure to look on evil; you cannot tolerate wrong." This speaks to the holiness of God. Other prophets, like Isaiah, had spoken to the people about the holiness of God, and Habakkuk built on that here.

Habakkuk compared the oppressed people of Judah to defenseless fish caught in the net of the wicked, unable to get free, completely at their mercy.

Rather than acknowledge God as provider and source of what they have, Babylon worshipped the tools of their conquest – they lived in luxury at the expense of those they conquered. They worshipped their own strength and military might rather than the God of creation.

Habakkuk had cried out to God, and now he moved to wait expectantly for God's response. Stephen Miller says, "Like a sentinel perched high in his watchtower scanning the horizon for signs of an enemy army, the prophet stood ready with great anticipation to hear what God would say to him."[4]

Habakkuk would wait. He had said all that was in his mind to say, and now he waited to hear how God would respond to his questions. He had been patient and persistent, and now he would wait.

We can relate to the idea of waiting, right? We spend much of our lives in that endeavor. From traffic lights to doctors' offices, from lines at the store to the hold music when we call a business, we know about waiting. Waiting is difficult. And we see the prophet waiting now, expectantly listening for the answer that he believes will come.

Before we move on to God's response to Habakkuk, let's look at a few observations from Habakkuk's prayer.

a. God is still sovereign. I know we covered this in the first part of this chapter, but I think it's worth mentioning again. Page Kelley says, "God does not allow His deeds and purposes to be controlled by persons, not even by righteous persons. He is and remains the sovereign Lord, always free to act unhindered, whether in judgment or in mercy...God will not be coerced to speak. Habakkuk could only be prepared to receive the Word of the Lord when it came; there was no way He could command it."[5]

We can't make God speak to us. I know that sounds trite and obvious, but it is a truth that we need to understand. God is sovereign; He will do what He will do according to His time and plan. He acts unhindered by people, in judgment or in mercy.

Habakkuk couldn't understand how God, in His holiness and purity, could see the evil and wickedness and not act. He saw God's not acting as implicit approval, but he knew that was inconsistent with who God is. So he went to God and asked Him. And God chose to answer Him directly.

b. Righteousness is not subjective. Do you know what I think Habakkuk's real problem with God's answer was? I think that Habakkuk was practicing comparative righteousness.

Comparative righteousness is essentially comparing ourselves with others and judging our righteousness against theirs. Think of it like this: we might see Mother Teresa or Billy Graham as very righteous people, and we see Adolf Hitler or Attila the Hun as very unrighteous people. Say there's a graph where you "rank" those people based on their righteousness. Now, where would you place yourself? We tend to compare ourselves to others that we know or know about and evaluate our level of righteousness compared to them. Sounds good, right?

The problem with comparative righteousness is that it's not Scriptural. Scripture says that there are none righteous, not even one. We look at some contemporary godly people and we think of them as righteous people, but in fact they are sinners just like us. One sin makes us a sinner – period. Like a drop of food coloring in a glass of water, the water is no longer pure; it is impure.

Another problem with comparative righteousness is that if we compare ourselves with people worse than us, we tend to feel pretty good about ourselves. We think that we're doing pretty well and even that God is lucky to have us on His team! We're one of the good guys! But Scripture says something different: all have sinned and fallen short of the glory of God. We've <u>all</u> fallen short. God looks at us and He sees a sinner, no more, no less. And since God cannot look on evil, we cannot be in His presence; we will spend eternity apart from Him, separated from our Creator forever.

But wait! God saw this and He desired that we be with Him, so He made a way. He sent one who had no sin, His Son Jesus the Messiah, the chosen one of God, to come and to suffer the punishment for our sin so that our account could be marked paid in full! So now all we who accept Christ and accept the payment that He made on our behalf can approach God. And now when He looks at us, He sees not our sin, but the righteousness of Jesus.

The biggest problem with comparative righteousness is that it's all about us. It's all about our actions and how we earn God's approval and the status of "righteous." This was the attitude of the Pharisees in Jesus' day, and Jesus attacked it head on. He told the story of a Pharisee (recorded in Luke 18:11) who came to pray and saw a sinner who was also praying, and he said **"thank you God that I am not like other men – robbers, evildoers, adulterers – or even like this tax collector here."** In other words, thanks, God, that I'm not a sinner like this guy!" That's comparative righteousness; that's what Habakkuk was using when he said that Babylon could not possibly judge Judah because Judah was much more righteous that Babylon was. And that's what we use when we compare ourselves to others and feel good (or bad) about ourselves.

The bottom line is that **our righteousness is found only in Jesus Christ, not in what we do.** What we do – our service to God and His church for Kingdom purposes – we don't do to earn "righteous points." We do what we do out of a heart of gratitude for all that God has done for us. We serve our King out of love and gratitude, not out of a desire to earn what we have received. It's just not possible to earn it – no way, no how.

GOD RESPONDS ONCE MORE

Habakkuk's waiting pays off; God responds once more, speaking directly to Habakkuk's main problem of comparative righteousness, and Habakkuk speaks no more in the book after this.

"Then the Lord replied: "Write down the revelation and make it plain on tablets so that a herald may run with it." Write it down. What great wisdom is captured here! I've said for many years that if I don't write down something that comes to mind, it never happens. God tells Habakkuk to write down what He's saying, I believe both for preservation and clarity. He wants to make sure this message is not forgotten or misunderstood.

"The revelation awaits an appointed time." God will set the timing, not Habakkuk, not the first hearers of his prophecy, and not us.

Then in verse four, we have the great contrast, between the unrighteous and the righteous. The ancient rabbis showed their regard for this passage by observing that Moses gave the people of Israel six hundred and thirteen commandments in Torah (the first 5 books of the Old Testament). David reduced them to 10 (Psalm 15); Isaiah to 6 (Isa. 33:15-16); Micah to 3 (Micah 6:8); Isaiah to 2 (Isa. 56:1); and Habakkuk to 1 (v. 4): **"the righteous person will live by his faithfulness."**

The righteous – that's one who intentionally conforms to the law of the Lord, who does what God says and follows His ways.

Will live – real, abundant life, not just the shadow counterfeit that this world offers. What God offers is the real thing, abundant, now and forever.

By his faithfulness – by fidelity and steadfastness. It's a picture of trust that endures. Do we obey God only when we understand the how and why, when it makes sense to us, or do we obey Him no matter what?

The apostle Paul taught this, that salvation comes by grace through faith alone (Romans 1:17, Galatians 3:11).

This became the rallying cry of the Protestant Reformation in the 16th century: "Sola Fides," faith alone.

Faithfulness means that believers commit themselves unreservedly to God and regard Him as absolutely trustworthy. The word is inclusive of the concepts of trust and obedience.

God will continue in chapter three of Habakkuk, explaining to Habakkuk that the evil of the Babylonians will be judged. God is just, and just as He is now judging the people of Judah, so too He will eventually judge the people of Babylon. And the book ends with a statement of God's ultimate sovereignty: **"The Lord is in his holy temple; let all the earth be silent before him."**

My final principle for leaders from Habakkuk is this: **You are not the ultimate King of the Universe**.

Shocking, I know! But in all seriousness, don't we leaders sometimes act as though everything in the universe hangs on what we do or say? Guess what: the Lord is in His holy temple. I am not God. God is on His throne. I am not.

I believe true humility comes from a right understanding of who God is and a right understanding of who we are. When we "super" size our perspective on ourselves, we get a skewed understanding of reality and think we're better than we are. When we minimize ourselves, we get a skewed perspective of reality and think we're worse than we are. But when we right size our perspective on ourselves and we understand and "right size" God in our minds, our perspective will be one of humility. And is there any greater leadership than that born from humility?

PRINCIPLES FROM HABAKKUK:

- Our questions can reveal our perspective.
- God is loving and sovereign, and we find our trust and hope solely in Him.
- Sin is never overlooked by God; it must be dealt with.
- You are not the ultimate King of the Universe.

7 HOSEA

"For I desire mercy, not sacrifice, and acknowledgement of God rather than burnt offerings."

--Hosea 6:6

"Is there a word from the Lord?"

The people of the northern nation of Israel began their nation in rebellion against Rehoboam, the son of Solomon. For the next two hundred years, NONE of the kings of the northern nation of Israel followed God. Not one. There is an element of the axiom here that a work birthed in sin and rebellion will not prosper. The people refused to submit to the son of Solomon, and in their rebellion they never saw God bless their efforts. In all that time, only one of the writing prophets prophesied to the northern nation of Israel: the prophet Hosea.

As we begin, it's important to remember again what I've said several times in this book. Modern readers of the Bible see prophecy as telling what's going to happen in the future; that's not what the vast majority of prophecy was in the time of the Old Testament. Prophets are better thought of as "covenant enforcers," men and women who spoke on behalf of God, telling the people the messages that He had for them. One of the most common commands by the prophets was "remember" – remember what God has done. Remember the covenant that God made with us. Remember the promises God made of His blessing when we follow Him, and remember the curses that He foretold would happen when we choose not to follow Him. This was the message of the prophets by and large, and while each one was unique, there was a thread of continuity among them around that idea.

Hosea's prophecy begins by telling us that he prophesied under the reign of Jeroboam, son of Jehoash. This was in the 8th century B.C.E., one that began with the nation of Israel in a time of peace and prosperity, but would not end that way. In the second half of the 8th century, the nation of Assyria had begun to rise to their east. Tiglath-Pilesar III took the throne in 745 B.C.E., and he threatened the northern nation of Israel when king Jeroboam aligned with the king of Syria in what we know as the Syro-Ephraimite War in 734 B.C.E. The southern nation of Judah refused to join their rebellious alliance, but instead aligned herself with Assyria against the rebels. The rebellion was ultimately crushed by Assyria in 722 B.C.E., with the destruction of Samaria, the capital of Israel, and the forced deportation of the people of Israel. The northern nation would not return to exist as a people again.

Though the 8th century began as a time of prosperity and decadence for many people, many others lived in destitute poverty. The prophets as a whole spoke often to the economic inequity among the people, where those who had enough and some to spare refused to share with their brothers who did not. This was not the way God designed their society to work, and the prophets spoke to that frequently, urging the people to remember that every life matters, and that God desired that a heart and spirit of generosity live among His people.

Hosea's name, which means "salvation," is the same Hebrew root word as in the names Isaiah, Joshua, and Jesus. Hosea lived at the same time as several other of the writing prophets, men like Isaiah, Amos, and Micah. Many scholars believe that Hosea was likely called to be a prophet as an older teenager, during a time when idolatry was rampant and syncretism was the norm. Syncretism, the blending of different belief systems and practices, was an ever present temptation to the people of Israel and Judah. Far too often, the people "hedged their bets" and added the worship of Ba'al to the worship of Yahweh, combining the methods of worship that God had laid out in the Mosaic Law with the traditional worship practices of the Canaanites and other pagan peoples.

It is into this time and place that God sent His message to His people through Hosea.

When Hosea first heard a word from God, he must have thought he'd lost his mind and completely misunderstood.

"The Lord said to him, "Go, marry a promiscuous woman and have children with her, for like an adulterous wife this land is guilty of unfaithfulness to the Lord."

What?? There's no way, God – really?? This doesn't make sense.

I believe Hosea's assignment was one of the toughest assignments in all of the Old Testament. He was told to do something completely out of the ordinary in order to drive home a message from God. That's known as a prophetic "speech-act." We see examples of this among other prophets: Isaiah walked around naked and barefoot for three years as a sign to the people of the coming exile of Egypt. Ezekiel lay on his side for over a year near a small model of Jerusalem under siege, and he was also forbidden to mourn when his wife died. Jeremiah did not marry.

All of these were acts that had a strong symbolic meaning to the people to whom the prophet was preaching.

I believe God began with this assignment, in essence asking Hosea, "Will you trust me? Will you walk in obedience to me, even when it doesn't make sense and you don't understand?"

Hosea stepped up and did what God asked; the text tells us that **"he married Gomer daughter of Diblaim, and she conceived and bore him a son."**

Children were seen as a sign of God's blessing; in the book of Hosea, they also served as part of the prophetic message. Note with me that the text says that Gomer bore "him" a son; that's going to be important later.

God told Hosea what to name the baby. Names in Scripture are often fraught with meaning, and this one is no exception. God said,

"Call him Jezreel, because I will soon punish the house of Jehu for the massacre at Jezreel, and I

will put an end to the kingdom of Israel. In that day I will break Israel's bow in the Valley of Jezreel."

The child's name was a symbol, a part of Hosea's prophecy to the people. It communicated that the people of Israel would soon be punished. They had trusted in military power and political power, not in the power of God, and their misplaced trust backfired on them. Judgment was coming.

The text continues:

"Gomer conceived again and gave birth to a daughter. Then the Lord said to Hosea, "Call her Lo-Ruhamah (which means "not loved"), for I will no longer show love to Israel, that I should at all forgive them. Yet I will show love to Judah; and I will save them—not by bow, sword or battle, or by horses and horsemen, but I, the Lord their God, will save them."

Note that the text doesn't say that Gomer bore Hosea a son, but just that she conceived and gave birth to a daughter. Most scholars believe, as do I, that this child was not Hosea's. Gomer had returned to her promiscuous ways, and her actions resulted in the birth of this second child.

God gave Hosea a name for this child too: Lo-Ruhamah, which means, "not loved." What a terrible name for a little girl! This name is a symbolic name again, telling the people of Israel that God will withdraw His love from Israel, just as He promised to do in Exodus 33 and Deuteronomy 7 if they were not faithful to the covenant with Him. Yet even in the midst of such dire judgment, there are grace notes. God mentions forgiveness, showing love to Judah, and saving them, not by military might, but by His power. And so He did. In 722 B.C.E., and again in 701 B.C.E., Assyria began to move south to wipe out Judah as they had done Israel, but God miraculously defended His people, and the Assyrians returned home. God keeps His promises – always.

We continue with Hosea and Gomer's story:

"After she had weaned Lo-Ruhamah, Gomer had another son. Then the Lord said, "Call him Lo-Ammi (which means "not my people"), for you are not my people, and I am not your God.

Once more, we see that Gomer had another son; the text doesn't say that she bore him to Hosea, leaving open the possibility (probability in my mind) that this child is not Hosea's either. I believe Gomer was continuing in her unfaithful ways, and again a child resulted.

God gave Hosea a name for the third child too: Lo-Ammi, meaning "not my people." God has declared that the people of Israel are not His people, and He is not their God. This is a statement of the breaking of the covenant that went back to Abraham, Isaac, and Jacob, a covenant that God would take Israel as His people and He would be their God. No more.

How tragic and heartbreaking this message must have been to Hosea, and how difficult it must have been for him to convey to the people of Israel. We have no indication that they listened or even cared, but to one who loved God and served as His prophet, this message must have been devastating.

And yet even in the midst of the worst message Hosea could imagine, there are again grace notes. "Yet" – the punishment would be for a limited time. There would again come a day when they would be the people of God. We hear echoes of the Abrahamic promise in these verses, and Hosea once again has hope. The first verse of chapter 2 says, **"Say of your brothers, 'My people,' and of your sisters, 'My loved one.'"** The names have been reversed; there is hope of restoration, even amidst such dark days and words of judgment!

Through the remainder of chapter two, we read the words of Hosea, responding to all that has happened so far. He refers to Gomer as "not my wife." He knows that there has been unfaithfulness and that has to wound him to the core. And yet... his response is not typical. In that day, a charge of adultery would have resulted in Gomer's being stoned, but we don't see Hosea making a public charge against her. Hosea knows that she has worshipped idols and even used his financial resources to do so; to this he could have responded with a public charge, again resulting in her death, but we don't see his doing that either.

Instead, we observe a blending of perspectives. See, this is not just the story of Hosea and Gomer; it's also the story of God and Israel. Hosea showed Gomer love, and she responded with unfaithfulness. God likewise showed Israel love, and she responded to Him with unfaithfulness. Chapter two, while it appears at first to be about Hosea and Gomer, is really all about God and His people.

Starting in verse fourteen, we see something surprising. God will pursue reconciliation with His people. In that verse, God says, **"Therefore I am now going to allure her; I will lead her into the wilderness and speak tenderly to her."**

What? Really? If anyone had grounds for divorce, it would be God. The people of Israel had broken the covenant repeatedly, and apparently intended to continue doing so. There was no remorse; there were no attempts at reconciliation from their side; there was only continued disobedience.

And yet God, in His unfathomable mercy and grace, chooses to pursue reconciliation with His people. He would have been well within His rights under the covenant to break it off with Israel, but He chooses the path of love, not "rights."

Let that sink in for a minute, in light of your own relationships. God chooses the path of love, not of "rights." What a powerful example for you and me. So difficult, so hard, and yet this is the path God would have us take every time in our own relationships. He set the example for us.

The people have chosen idols, time and time again, and there will be punishment for their actions. Reconciliation doesn't mean the avoidance of all consequences. They have forgotten that God, not Ba'al, is the source of all blessings (2:8). God tells them that He will take away blessings, expose the sin, and stop the celebrations and feasts.

There were three annual Jewish feasts: Passover, the Feast of Weeks or Firstfruits, and the Feast of Booths or Tabernacles. The celebration known as new moons happened monthly, and Sabbath days were weekly celebrations reminding Israel of God's rest in creation and of Israel's experience as slaves in Egypt. Apparently the people had continued celebrating all of these festivals and special days, but they had forgotten the reason they did: the Lord God Himself (2:13).

The first two chapters of Hosea are difficult, but they tell us several things that I believe leaders need to take to heart. The first is this: **Tough assignments are not a sign of God's displeasure; they indicate His faith in us.**

God didn't give this assignment to Hosea because of his sin. He didn't give it to Hosea because He didn't like him very much. He gave it to Hosea because He had faith in Hosea. He had faith that Hosea would follow Him even when it hurt, even when it didn't make sense, even when other people had to be telling him to cut his losses and get out of such a marriage.

197

In the prophecy of Hosea, I believe we also see that **God takes sin <u>very</u> seriously.** He doesn't wink at it (Deuteronomy 4:23-31). God will not accept second place in the lives of His people; He will not be one of many gods in their lives or ours. Sin is sin, and God takes it seriously; whether it's gossip or murder, whether it's rebellion or anger, God takes it very seriously. There are no "respectable" or "acceptable" sins in His eyes.

God's desire for His people, then and now, is that we would trust Him and walk in obedience to His Word. That phrase "the word of the Lord" appears four hundred and thirty eight times in the Old Testament! God lets His people know His message; the problem lies in a people who refuse to accept it and obey it. Too often, we are educated beyond our level of obedience. Most of us don't need another Bible study; we need to be obedient to what we know already. God loves us as we are, but He never leaves us as we are. God desires that no one would perish, but that all would come to life with Him.

1 Peter 2:9-10 gives us a New Testament echo of Hosea, a promise for all who follow God:

"But you are a chosen people, a royal priesthood, a holy nation, God's special possession, that you may declare the praises of him who called you out of darkness into his wonderful light. Once you were not a people, but now you are the people of God; once you had not received mercy, but now you have received mercy."

Idolatry is as much a temptation today as it was in Hosea's day, and from the first two chapters of Hosea we see that **God will not tolerate <u>anything</u> taking His rightful place in our lives.**

As it was in the days of Hosea, idolatry is wrong, and God doesn't excuse it. He takes our relationship with Him very seriously, and we would be wise to do the same. We can be just as unfaithful to God as the people of Israel, and in some ways more so, as we have the benefit of His written Word, the Bible; we have an abundance of blessings in our lives that are far too easy to take for granted.

God's invitation to the people of Israel is the same as the invitation He offers to you and me today: return to Me. He desires reconciliation; that's why He sent us Jesus! Leader, turn away from trusting in yourself, and turn to Him, trusting Him completely and walking in full obedience to His Word. Reject the idols and by the power of God's Spirit, refocus your life on Him and Him alone. Realize that every blessing comes from Him; every good gift comes from Him. Don't forget Him in the words and actions of your everyday life; remember Whose you are, and live your life for an Audience of One who loves you with an everlasting love.

THE VALLEY OF ACHOR

Have you ever done something stupid and wrong? Have you been forgiven of it but still find it hard to forget, to put it out of your mind? We tend to have long memories of the past, of our sin and failure. In the next part of Hosea, we're going to see God speak to that very situation.

I want to focus on two verses in particular in chapter two, verses fourteen and fifteen:

"Therefore I am now going to allure her; I will lead her into the wilderness and speak tenderly to her. There I will give her back her vineyards, and will make the Valley of Achor a door of hope. There she will respond as in the days of her youth, as in the day she came up out of Egypt."

In this section, God begins to turn toward reconciliation, and we begin to move from judgment to restoration. "Give back her vineyards," for instance, is a reversal of the judgment declared in 2:12. But then Hosea mentions the Valley of Achor. What is that?

The Valley of Achor is tied to the events of Joshua 7. When the people of Israel, under Joshua's leadership, began to move into the Promised Land, they first encountered Jericho. God fought for them, and the city was destroyed. The people were given very specific instructions not to claim any of the plunder of Jericho for themselves, but instead to devote it all to destruction as an act of worship and gratitude to God for what He had done. All the people obeyed except one, a man named Achan. Achan took some of the plunder for his own, unbeknownst to any of the other people of Israel, and he hid it under his tent.

Next they came to the city of Ai, and the people were utterly confident. Some of the men told Joshua that it wouldn't even take the whole army to go out this time. Joshua agreed and sent out a smaller contingent, but instead of victory, the people were routed! What happened?

Joshua went in prayer to God, asking Him that very thing. And God responded by telling Joshua what had been done; someone had taken some of the plunder of Jericho, thus bringing sin into the camp. God takes sin seriously.

Joshua immediately went out, sought out who had done this thing, and found Achan out. When Joshua confronted him, Achan confessed to taking a robe, two hundred shekels of silver, and a bar of gold weighing fifty shekels and hiding them under his tent. Joshua sent someone to get the plunder, and it was brought back and laid out before all the people and God.

Joshua then commanded that everything that belonged to Achan and his family was to be all put into one big area, and then he and all of his family and possessions were to be stoned, burned, and then covered over with a large pile of rocks. That place became known, even hundreds and hundreds of years later in the days of Hosea, as the Valley of Achor, which means valley of trouble, because of the trouble that Achan brought on the people of Israel in that place.

Why would Hosea mention that here?

Because God is a God who turns failure into hope.

God said through Hosea: **"I will make the Valley of Achor a door of hope."** What they saw as a place of shame and failure, God would redeem and make into a door of hope through which they could walk into a new day. They had a long memory of failure associated with the name Achor. God would take that memory and transform it into a name associated with hope.

In chapter 2, we see God using the imagery of marriage for his relationship with His people. Israel will call Him "my husband" (2:16); they will be betrothed (2:19) in righteousness, justice, love, compassion, and faithfulness. What a beautiful picture of the love of God! And it is here in Hosea that we first see the basis for the New Testament concept of the church as the bride of Christ.

In the end, God will again show His love to His people. In verse 23 God says,

"I will show my love to the one I called 'Not my loved one. I will say to those called 'Not my people,' 'You are my people'; and they will say, 'You are my God.'"

Hosea is told in 3:1-3 to **"go, show your love to your wife <u>again</u>."** And we begin to understand the cost and the magnitude of an "again" kind of love, a love that is chosen after unfaithfulness, after sin, after brokenness, and after reconciliation. That "again" kind of love is completely unearned and is always costly.

Hosea is told by God to go and get Gomer.

Apparently she had sold herself into slavery, and Hosea would have to buy her out of that. It's recorded that he paid fifteen shekels of silver and a homer and a lethek of barley. A normal slave price at this time was thirty shekels of silver. It could very well be that Hosea didn't have enough silver to get her, so he had to throw in the barley too. It cost him greatly.

Can you imagine what must have been going through his mind? What if she runs off again? What if she doesn't want to come home? What if the love I thought we shared is dead? What if the rest of our lives we'll live under the same roof with that memory?

And yet we see him simply put into action his love for God and his wife. In 3:2, he says, "I bought her." No record of hesitation, no record of second thoughts. It's just simple obedience to what God told him to do.

He tells Gomer that she's going to come home with him where she will no longer live a lifestyle of promiscuity, but will live in their home with him for many days.

Can you imagine what she must have been thinking when she saw Hosea? She might have been expecting words of rebuke, something to the effect of "so this is how far you've fallen – selling yourself into slavery." But instead, she is shown love and mercy and forgiveness. She had earned none of that, yet it is extended to her.

Hosea then prophesies of the exile when the people of Israel will live many days without a king in another land – but it will not be for forever. At the end of the appointed time, the people will return and seek God as well as David their king. The people of Israel had rebelled against the household of David, broken away, and formed their own nation; after the exile, there will be a coming together of the people of God under the leadership of His appointed king.

Willem Van Gemeren says of this passage, "True repentance calls for submission to the Lord and also to the Lord's anointed king. It was not enough to live by one portion of God's revelation and to reject another... God had given his revelation through Moses at Mt Sinai and he had given his rule on earth through a Davidic king...

people may not enter into the era of restoration unless they completely abandon their former ways, submit to God, and express loyalty to the Davidic King of Kings, the Messiah."[1]

Several things I think leaders can take away from this section of Hosea.

a) Obedience to God is not a buffet line.

That sounds trite, but I mean it. We don't get to pick and choose what part of God's commands we will obey! When God tells us to do something, we're to do that. Unfortunately I believe many people treat obedience to God like a buffet line: "I'll do that, but not that; sure, some of that, but not going near that." God's clear with the people of Israel that it's an all-or-nothing covenant.

b) Reconciliation always costs everyone involved.

Reconciliation with Gomer cost Hosea financially, emotionally, and legally. I'm sure some of the people around him reminded him of his rights in this situation — he was the injured spouse! And yet reconciliation meant more to him than his rights.

Reconciliation with Hosea cost Gomer her pride. She had to go home knowing all that she had done and knowing that she had done nothing to earn Hosea's love, mercy, or forgiveness.

Reconciliation with God cost Israel her obedience and her pride too. She also had to come understanding all that she had done and knowing that she had done nothing to earn God's love, mercy, or forgiveness.

Incidentally, you and I come to God the same way.

And reconciliation with Israel cost God the most of all. It cost Him his "rights" under the covenant, and the ultimate reconciliation with humanity would cost Him His Son, Jesus.

Gomer forfeited her right to Hosea's love; God tells him to give it anyway. This will be a symbol that despite

Israel's unfaithfulness, God will offer reconciliation anyway.

Reconciliation is not earned. God shows His love and mercy not because we deserve it, but because we need it and because of who He is.

c) As long as you're still breathing, failure is not final.

God says He will make the valley of Achor into a door of hope! God can take the place and symbol of our greatest shame and failure and make it into a door that leads into a future beyond what we could ever hope for or imagine.

The basic statement of the covenant with Abraham, Isaac, and Jacob was "I will be your God and you will be my people." As Paul teaches us in Romans 8:31, God is <u>for</u> us! Satan, the adversary, will remind us of our sin and failure, but we have to remember what Scripture says — what Jesus said — "it is finished."

We all have our own valley of Achor, our memories of sin and failure. The One who offered a door of hope to Israel came in Jesus Christ to be that door for you and me. Jesus said in John 10:9-10,

"I am the door; if anyone enters through Me, he will be saved, and will go in and out and find pasture. The thief comes only to steal and kill and destroy; I came that they may have life, and have it abundantly."

Achan willfully did what he knew was wrong, just as Israel did and just as we do. Our tendency when we see that we are wrong and are found out is to try to work our way out of the situation. We want to do it all by ourselves, and say "I did it my way," rather than sing God's song (see Exodus 15 for the lyrics).

God did not give up on His people. He wouldn't let Hosea give up on his bride. His desire is to express that "again" kind of love to every person He created, including you. He has not changed.

Romans 5:8 says, **"But God demonstrates his own love for us in this: While we were still sinners, Christ died for us."**

You don't have to get your life cleaned up first. You don't have to make sure everything is right in your life before God will accept you. His desire is to express that "again" kind of love to every person, no matter where you've been or what you've done. As long as you're still breathing, failure is not final

JUSTICE AND RESTORATION

I remember that when I was in college there was a big trial going on that was everywhere on the news: the trial of OJ Simpson for the murder of his wife and the man she was involved with. After a long trial, the jury came back and gave the verdict: not guilty.

In March 2012, the former governor of Illinois, Rod Blagojevich, who was removed from office through impeachment, began his prison sentence after being found guilty on eighteen counts of federal corruption charges.

These two cases were very high profile. One man found innocent, one man found guilty.

I think it's true that most people want to see justice done; that's a big deal to us. We want to see the guilty punished and the righteous rewarded. When that happens, we feel that all is right with the world.

In the remainder of the book of Hosea, we find the issues of justice and restoration occurring again and again. Hosea's prophecy is full of principles that I believe can benefit each of us, and I want to zero in on some of those as we look at chapters 4-14.

a) Leadership is critical, and God holds leaders accountable. (4:1-9)

God speaks to the corruption and poor leadership of the priests. These were the men who were supposed to be representing God, making sure that worship happened appropriately and that justice was done, but somewhere along the way, they forgot Whom they served and, instead, began to serve their own interests.

Leadership is critical. As the leaders go, so go the people. We see that in Hosea's day among the people of Israel, and we see it in our day as well.

If leaders lead well and the people following them see that, then they will have confidence and a measure of trust. It's just like the author of Hebrews tells us in Hebrews 13:17:

"Have confidence in your leaders and submit to their authority, because they keep watch over you as those who must give an account. Do this so that their work will be a joy, not a burden, for that would be of no benefit to you."

When leaders don't lead well, God's Word is clear that He will hold them accountable. The priests of Hosea's day came before God and faced Him with all that they had done, and leaders today must remember that we will be held accountable by God for what we say and how we lead.

Paul wrote to the church at Rome, **"to those who have been given the spiritual gift of leadership, lead with all diligence"** (Romans 12:9); he didn't mean just when it's easy or just when you feel like it.

I think one of the greatest prayers in the Bible for a leader is found in 2 Chronicles 1:10. Solomon prayed, **"Give me wisdom and knowledge, that I may lead this people, for who is able to govern this great people of yours?"** As a leader, that has been my prayer so often – wisdom and knowledge. So many days, I feel as though I'm not up to the task of leading God's people. So many days, I feel as though I'm not wise enough or knowledgeable enough to lead well. As did Solomon, I come to God, the source of all wisdom and knowledge, asking for what is needed to lead His people well.

In the pages of Scripture, we see good leadership decisions and practices from men like Solomon, Nehemiah (Nehemiah 6), and Joshua (Joshua 1). We also see bad leadership decisions from men like Aaron (in Exodus 32) and Nadab and Abihu (Leviticus 10).

Over and over, we are reminded that leadership is critical, and God holds leaders accountable.

b) Arrogance and pride can lead to a hardened rebellion that refuses to change because it means an admission of guilt. (5:1-6, 7:10)

Sin is rebellion against God (5:2). And not calling on God (7:7,14) or not turning to Him is the ultimate snub of defiance (7:10,14,16). And closely associated with it, from the same passages in Hosea,

c) A teachable spirit is not optional, especially for leaders.

God has given us His Word to teach us, inspire us, and encourage us. Romans 15:4 says,

"For everything that was written in the past was written to teach us, so that through the endurance taught in the Scriptures and the encouragement they provide we might have hope."

If leaders forget to be continual learners and, instead, develop an attitude of arrogance and pride thinking they know it all, then their hearts will become hardened. They will refuse to change because that would mean that they were wrong. This is exactly the situation of the royal house of Israel in Hosea's day. It's also the situation of too many leaders in our own day as well.

Leaders MUST model a teachable heart and a teachable spirit. By doing so, we will reject the attitudes of arrogance and pride that so displease God and cause other people to become repelled by our leadership. It's not always easy – in fact, it's often very difficult – but it's not optional for a leader who leads with all diligence.

I can think of many times when, as a leader, I chose poorly and did not always listen with a teachable spirit. Too often, I was more concerned about what I wanted, what I was going to say next, how I was going to 'one up' the discussion and 'win' the argument. But in doing so, I found that I trampled on the feelings and dreams of others – that's no way to lead. Leaders MUST model a teachable heart and spirit.

d) It's all about the heart. (5:15-6:6)

The people's half-hearted repentance and seeking of God is not enough (5:15-6:6); only following God with all their heart, all their soul, all their mind, and all their strength would suffice.

True revival changes you forever.

How many times have you seen someone who gets "on fire" for following God, only to have that fire diminish into ashes in days or weeks? How many times have you seen someone make an emotion-based decision to choose God, only to see that decision go by the wayside when the emotion passes? That's not what Hosea is talking about here; he's talking about a true revival of the heart that lasts beyond the moment, beyond the emotion.

Hosea teaches the people that true worship involves both the way people praise God in His house AND the way they live their daily lives (10:11-13). It's all about the heart.

Hoses 6:6 is one of the cornerstone verses from this book. The NIV translates it: **"For I desire mercy, not sacrifice, and acknowledgement of God rather than burnt offerings."** The NLT says, **"I want you to show love, not offer sacrifices. I want you to know me more than I want burnt offerings."** The Message paraphrases it: **"I'm after love that lasts, not more religion. I want you to know God, not go to more prayer meetings."** I love that. And there we can see the heart of this verse and this book – it's all about the heart!

e) **There is hope beyond judgment based on who God is (11:1-11, 14:1-9).**

I believe that verses 1-11 of chapter 11 are a window into the heart of God. He does not let infatuation or bitterness govern His decisions; His love is far greater than the emotional turmoil we experience and associate with love.

Over and over in this book, we find the idea of hope. Hope is offered when it is not deserved; hope is promised in the midst of failure; hope is seen in the darkest of judgment days. In that hope we see restoration coming after repentance like a rainbow comes after a storm (14:1-9). The people of Israel would eventually raise their white flags of surrender to God (14:3), and there would be no more trusting in anything or anyone other than God. Hosea encouraged them to "take words with you and return to the Lord." Bring your words as an offering as you return to God, but make sure your words reflect your heart and your actions.

I want to close this chapter with three questions that I think would be helpful as we finish out our look at the message of Hosea.

If I'm a follower of Jesus, have I wandered away from God as the people of Israel did? We have to own it if we have and "take words" (we don't come to God empty handed; take words of genuine repentance that reflect your heart's decision).

In what is my trust? I must turn from my old ways of living and completely surrender to God's ways.

Am I bearing fruit spiritually? Is there current evidence of my life being transformed by God and bearing His fruit (Galatians 5:22-23)?

God offers unearned grace and mercy; what is my response?

The key to interpreting Hosea's message is not intelligence, but submission to God and His ways. That's real wisdom.

PRINCIPLES FROM HOSEA:

- Tough assignments are not a sign of God's displeasure; they indicate His faith in us.
- Obedience to God is not a buffet line.
- Reconciliation always costs everyone involved.
- As long as you're still breathing, failure is not final.
- Leadership is critical, and God holds leaders accountable.
- Arrogance and pride can lead to a hardened

rebellion that refuses to change because it means an admission of guilt.

- A teachable spirit is not optional, especially for leaders.

- It's all about the heart.

- There is hope beyond judgment based on who God is.

8 ZEPHANIAH

"As long as you are proud, you cannot know God. A proud man is always looking down on things and people; and, of course, as long as you are looking down you cannot see something that is above you."

--C.S. Lewis

If I had to summarize this book with a question, it would be this: what does God want from me?

Maybe that's a question you've had. I think at one time or another, and maybe pretty frequently, we're asking that question: what does God want from me? That's a big question, and one worth exploring and answering if we can. I believe Zephaniah was written in part to help us do that.

Zephaniah's prophetic career likely took place in the 630's B.C.E. Less than a century before, in 722 B.C.E., the Assyrian kings Shalmanesar I and Sargon II had destroyed Samaria, the capital of the northern nation of Israel. They then turned their attention southward, eyeing the nation of Judah, and began moving to invade and destroy her. But the king of Judah, Hezekiah, cried out to God, seeking Him in that day, and God miraculously intervened. The Assyrian army was turned back and returned home to Nineveh.

After Hezekiah's death, Judah had two kings who sadly did not follow the ways of God, Manasseh and Ammon. Manasseh reigned for fifty-five years, and Ammon reigned for two years. During this time, the nation of Judah sank deeply into idolatry, following these godless leaders into practices that greatly displeased God. After Ammon's death, eight-year-old Josiah came to the throne. He loved God and led the people of Judah for thirty-one years, from 640-609 B.C.E. It was during his reign that the book of the Law, probably Deuteronomy, was "rediscovered" in the Temple where it had lain languishing for nearly sixty years. After hearing the words of the Law, Josiah knew what he had to do. He began reforms in Jerusalem and in all of Judah.

It had been seventy years since the last prophetic word from God had come through the prophet Isaiah, who tradition records was put to death by Manasseh. Into this time in Judah's history came the prophet Zephaniah.

Zephaniah, whose name means "the Lord hides" or "the Lord protects," lived at the same time as Jeremiah, Habakkuk, and Nahum. He was of royal heritage, the great, great grandson of Hezekiah. He was probably in his early twenties when he began to prophesy and preach to the people of Judah.

We see a lot of intensity and urgency in Zephaniah's words. He begins his prophecy with a blunt message of judgment, preaching to the people before the finding of the Law in the Temple and the reforms instituted by

Josiah. He starts out saying that the worship of God among the people has been corrupted, and God's judgment is threatened. Just as Jonah did to Nineveh, Zephaniah preaches a message of impending judgment and destruction, but this time it's to come to the people of God.

The people have begun blending the worship of God and the worship practices of the Canaanites and the other people of the land (you'll remember we've already discussed that, a practice known as syncretism). Instead of following the instructions in the Mosaic Law, the people began to "add to" their worship, using ideas and methods that they had picked up from those nations around them. Apparently there had also been the worship of Ba'al, the storm god from Canaanite mythology. This was an ever present snare to the people; Ba'al and Asherah, the goddess of fertility, were often denounced in the preaching of the prophets because of the people's willingness to follow that temptation and worship those false gods either alongside or instead of the one true God. Worship had been corrupted.

They had not only worshipped these false gods of the Canaanites but had even begun worshipping the starry host. Astrology and idol worship were everywhere. This was the legacy of Manasseh and his son Ammon, who had led the people in these horrendous practices, and the people continued them even beyond the deaths of those wicked kings. They swore by Molech, a Canaanite false god to whom child sacrifices were offered in hopes of prosperity and stability.

Can you imagine fathers and mothers who sacrifice their children? Can you imagine giving your child up to such a fate, hoping as you do so that this will lead to increased financial security and stability? Who does that? These people did.

Syncretism is deadly, and Jesus spoke to it in Luke 16:13, **"no one can serve two masters."** The people believed in God, but that's not enough. James 2:19 tells us, **"You believe that there is one God. Good! Even the demons believe this and they tremble in terror."** There's a difference between believing in God and trusting in Him.

Zephaniah is warning two additional groups here: those who turn back from following the Lord (the faithless), and those who neither seek Him nor inquire of Him (the indifferent). He tells them that the Day of the Lord is near (v7-17).

God is angry in chapter 1 – why? The source of God's anger is not the outsider or the unbeliever, but the hypocrisies and betrayals of His own created, chosen, and rescued people. This is a very important point for the unbeliever, as this message is not directed at them.

This might bother you. You might not like seeing this picture of God, but we need to understand what's going on here. God's people have either rebelled against or ignored Him, and He takes both of those very, very seriously.

Zephaniah speaks of God's punishment and justice for

- those who practice superstitions,
- those engaged in idolatrous worship,
- those who unjustly treat and deal with others,
- the complacent,

- and the practical atheists – those who believe in God but who act daily as though He doesn't exist.

The Day of the Lord will be nothing like what they expect. It's coming quickly, and the people are not ready. God had warned them, in Deuteronomy 8:10-14, 17-19, but they did not listen. He had sent prophets to warn them and remind them, but they did not listen. He had told the people that their trust was misplaced (v.18); silver and gold could not save them.

Zephaniah used the expression "Day of the Lord" more than did any other prophet. His prophecy of destruction was confirmed by the prophetess Huldah (2 Kings 22:20) and was fulfilled in 587/586 B.C.E. with the destruction of Jerusalem and Judah.

Before we move on from chapter one of Zephaniah, let's look at a couple of things that leaders need to keep in mind from his prophecy.

a) God is just, not fair.

I've heard Andy Stanley say more than once, "Fairness ended in the Garden of Eden." Do we REALLY want God to be fair with us? Really? I don't think so. Fair means that we get what we deserve. Fair means that we pay the price for our sin and disobedience instead of accepting Jesus' sacrifice on our behalf. I don't want fair. But I do know that God is just.

b) God takes worship very, very seriously.

Worship is not just on Sunday mornings! Worship involves our entire lives. The church is where Heaven and Earth meet – where our prayer is that God's will would be done on earth as it is in Heaven. That's a tall order, and it happens only with committed Christ followers who are empowered by the Holy Spirit of God.

Worship is everyday life. It's as much what happens in your office and on the streets of your city or in your home as what happens in a church building. The church building is no holier than your home, your kitchen, or your bathroom; God is present everywhere and sees it all.

Practical atheism is not OK for a follower of Jesus (believing in God but acting daily as though He does not exist) because God is passionate about the worship of His people. The problem behind the idolatry and superstition of the people in Zephaniah's day is the focus of their trust and worship. They are proud and arrogant, and they trust in themselves and their wealth. In our terminology, they're tidying up for Sunday worship, but the rest of their lives are untouched.

What does your lifestyle look life Monday through Saturday? What is the focus of your life and your heart?

Think for a moment about the path of your life, and think of where it will end (it will eventually). Think about your funeral, your tombstone; what would you like to be said and written about you? He was a millionaire? She was a successful businesswoman? He was the first one at the office and the last one to leave everyday? She never took time off? What does success look like for a follower of Jesus? What are the priorities we need to have in our lives?

c) God expects that the resources He gives His people will be used according to His commands, not as a source competing for the trust that is to be in Him alone.

Jesus told the religious people of His day not to neglect the tithe and to practice justice, mercy, and faithfulness (Matthew 23:23, Luke 11:42). They were still under the Law of Moses, and that covenant was based on their obedience. Justice and mercy mean helping the poor, the widow, the orphan, and the oppressed. You and I today live under a new covenant; we're not under the Law of Moses, and there is freedom in that. However, when we aren't good stewards of the resources He has entrusted to us, we take ourselves out from under His hand of blessing.

Paul wrote in 1 Timothy 6:10, **"For the love of money is a root of all kinds of evil. Some people, eager for money, have wandered from the faith and pierced themselves with many griefs."** That's why today in America, we see that 21% of church members and consistent attenders don't give anything to their church, and

71% give less than 2% of their income. How do you explain that in light of what God's Word says? It's a lack of trusting in God and doing what His Word says. It's trusting in what's in our pockets more than trusting in God.

Does that mean you have to rearrange your life? Yes! Trusting in God, accepting Jesus Christ, affects everything; we arrange our lives around what His Word teaches us.

My main principle for leaders from the first chapter of Zephaniah is this: **what you worship determines what you become.**

If you worship and seek after the things of this world, then you will become like this world – that's the path you're taking.

If you worship and seek after the things of God, you will become like Jesus – that's the path you're taking.

What are our idols today? We become just like them. Money, sex, success, power, prestige, the accumulation of stuff, image (both to ourselves and how we appear to others) – they're everywhere.

Did you know that at the January, 2013, presidential inauguration in Washington, D.C., the royal suite at the Georgetown Four Seasons hotel went for $20,000 per night? A 4,000 square foot suite. Tell me this – how many people in our world, in our community, could be impacted for $20,000? How many children that need sponsors through Compassion International could have their lives saved and changed forever with $20,000? What we do with the resources we have speaks to the god we worship. What we do with the resources we have speaks to whether we are followers of Jesus or just practical atheists.

Look at 2:3 – **"seek the Lord."** That reminds me of what Jesus said in Matthew 6:33, **"Seek His Kingdom and His righteousness"** – everything else, everybody else, will disappoint you and fail you. Only God is always good, always holy, always just, always right. Zephaniah is calling the people of Judah and the people of today to a life of humility, not pride, warning us all against trusting in anything other than God.

The focus of the heart is crucial. What you worship determines what you become.

Too many people are worshipping something other than God. Too many people have put their spouse, their career, their kids, money, sex, image, power, or something else in the place of priority that belongs only to God. And I'm talking to the church here; this is a message primarily to God's people, not those who are outside the community of faith.

God wants all of our lives, not just an hour or two on Sundays. He wants us to seek Him one hundred and sixty-eight hours a week. When we look at what we do with our time and our money, we need to see His presence there, His influence there, our obedience there, not our giving Him just tips of our time on Sundays or tips from the resources He entrusts to us. We need to understand that He has given us everything we have: our strength, our health, our money, our time. And He expects us to utilize every one of those for Him and His work. It's that simple.

That's what God wants because He knows that what we worship determines what we become. If you're still breathing, there's hope. You can turn away from what you've been doing and turn toward God who loves you more than you can imagine. That's the good news of the gospel: Jesus came to offer us rest from the striving of the Law. He offers us hope and a future with God, not separation from Him. Just as was true of the people of Judah though, the choice is ours.

SEEKING HUMILITY

God's judgment has been pronounced in chapter one; now what?

In 2:1, Zephaniah called the people **"shameful"** – literally the Hebrew means, "not to long for." The people have not stopped longing for things (1:13,18), but they have stopped longing for the Creator of all things. They were called a shameful "nation," but it's not the word for nation normally associated with God's people; it's the word goy, which is usually used of Gentile nations. What was going on?

Zephaniah was using every tool at his disposal to communicate to the people the most important message they could ever hear: Repent! While there was still time.

In these words of judgment, there are again grace notes. He spoke next to **"all you humble of the land,"** that is, those who abandoned the arrogance of their idolatry and wickedness to seek humility; those who in poverty of spirit relied on God rather than their own power or machinations for vindication. There was a remnant who had not followed the worship of Ba'al, people who had not bowed their knees in idolatry, but who loved and served the one true God.

What was this remnant (as well as all those who chose to join them!) supposed to do? Three things according to 2:3:

- Seek Yahweh, their covenant God
- Live godly lives, marked by practicing justice (do what He commands)
- Seek righteousness and further humility; practice submissive obedience to God

God's holiness and justice are not all He is, or else the totality of mankind would be lost. The fact that they are not destroyed arises from God's mercy, compassion, and love, which are an equal part of His being. Sin will lead to punishment; repentance and return to a covenant relationship with God will lead to salvation and restoration. The word "perhaps" safeguards God's sovereign freedom. Furthermore, we know that because God is always just and does what is right, in the face of true repentance there is no other response possible than forgiveness.

Zephaniah moved on to declare judgment on the nations around Judah (2:4-3:8): Philistia to their east, Moab and Ammon to their west, Cush (Egypt) to their south, and Assyria to their north. The nations will be judged for what they have done: for their pride, for their cruelty, and ultimately for declaring with Assyria, "there is none besides me." God will judge them, and they will be destroyed. Nineveh, the capital of Assyria, will be utterly desolate (2:13). Even the site of Nineveh was later forgotten until discovered through modern archaeological excavations. These words of judgment and destruction were meant to serve as a warning to the people of Judah to repent and turn back to God while they could.

After dealing with the nations around Judah, Zephaniah moved on to the city of Jerusalem, capital of Judah, and lamented because there was rebellion, defilement, and oppression there. What are they to repent of? Zephaniah lists 5 specific charges:

- She had not listened to the message of God as spoken through the prophets
- She obeyed no one, not even the Lord
- She had refused to accept discipline or correction
- She had not trusted God
- She had not drawn near to Him in penitent worship, the only One who could provide direction and guidance for her

The leaders were called out specifically in this. Officials, rulers, prophets, priests; all classes of leadership were castigated for indulging in conduct completely opposed to their vocations and responsibilities. No one was exempted, and the leaders least of all. Leaders are held to a higher standard, then and now.

Despite the failing of the people, God never fails (Lamentations 3:22-23). He declares His intent clearly in 3:8. **"Wait"** is sarcastic; often this verb has a positive connotation of expected blessing, but not here! Since an integral part of God's character is holiness and the inability to countenance sin, the depravity of man can be met only by His wrath.

Finally, Zephaniah moves to the remnant (2:7, 2:9b), those who had not fallen away from God but continued to follow Him. The remnant (who are also mentioned in Jeremiah, Amos, and Micah) is a symbol of hope; the promised judgment will not be total. It signifies both the severity of God's punishment and the graciousness of His mercy. Destruction will come, but not annihilation. Nothing can avert the doom on the nation (see the prophet Huldah's confirmation of Zephaniah's prophecy in 2 Kings 22:15-17), but genuine repentance may save the praying remnant. Repentance, however, must be manifested in works – seeking the Lord and doing what He commands.

Leaders, what can we see for us in this section of Zephaniah?

a) God is totally opposed to arrogance.

Zephaniah is a strong call for a self-absorbed culture to come back to reality. He is God; we are not.

b) If we're still breathing, there's an opportunity to turn back to God.

There is always a remnant. And God's grace is big enough to cover all of our sins.

Zephaniah is calling the people of Judah to a life of humility, not pride, warning them (and us) against trusting in anything other than God.

That's what God wants because He knows that what we worship determines what we become. And if we're still here, still breathing, there's still hope. **Prideful arrogance separates us from God; humility brings us closer to Him.**

Are we ever like the people of Judah? Absolutely. Think about how many times in the church we have refused to extend grace, sometimes over some really minor things. In seventeen years of ministry, I've seen prideful arrogance over everything from music to volume levels to styles of preaching to who will get spoken to in the hallway to what we say on Facebook or Twitter about others. The idea of prideful arrogance, refusing to offer grace, is not limited to any demographic; it's not limited to any segment of the population at all; it's a human condition problem with which we all wrestle.

The problem of arrogance and pride comes down to one thing – trust. Will I trust in my own opinions, what I know, what I like, or will I place my trust in God and what He says and leave handling other people up to Him?

My bottom line for leaders from this section of Zephaniah is this: **you can't look down on others when you're facedown in the dust.**

That is so countercultural, so different from the society and people around us. We're taught to stand with our head held high, pulling ourselves up by our bootstraps and not being dependent on anyone for anything. Many would resonate with the words of William Ernest Henley from *Invictus*, "I am the master of my fate, I am the captain of my soul." Be in charge, and don't be dependent on others. Leaders are supposed to be above the behavior of those who serve, right?

Wrong. That is not the experience of the follower of Jesus – it's just not. It's about humbling ourselves, face down before God, and from that position we can't look down on anyone else for anything.

In his classic book *Mere Christianity*, C.S. Lewis said, "As long as you are proud, you cannot know God. A proud man is always looking down on things and people;

and, of course, as long as you are looking down you cannot see something that is above you."

Do we want to truly know God? Do we want to seek Him like Zephaniah and Jesus encourage? Then it starts here, by humbling ourselves and putting ourselves last, putting our wants and our desires after those of others, and putting obedience to God first.

Being a disciple is not about doing everything our way until it doesn't work or gets hard and then firing up a flare prayer. Being a disciple of Jesus means doing what He says no matter what. When it doesn't make sense. When it does make sense. When it's hard. When it's easy. When it doesn't affect anyone but us. When it affects people all around us.

We have to get past this view of being a Christian that makes it all about a walk up an aisle and getting wet and that's it. It's WAY more than that. It's about a daily, conscious choice to follow Jesus. Jesus said it this way in Luke 9:23: **"Whoever wants to be my disciple must deny themselves and take up their cross daily and**

follow me." Deny yourself sounds to me a whole lot like humbling ourselves, like going facedown in the dust.

You can't look down on others when you're facedown in the dust. That's why God tells us His heart on this. This is what He wants for us, and it's so hard and challenging.

When we get this right – when we realize that it is in Jesus alone that we find hope, peace and life – then we discover the truth of what Zephaniah's telling us; that trusting in God is an all or nothing decision, and it begins with humility.

JUDGMENT OR GRACE?

Theologian Palmer Robertson says, "One of the most awesome descriptions of the wrath of God in judgment found anywhere in Scripture appears in the opening verses of Zephaniah… one of the most moving descriptions of the love of God for His people found anywhere in Scripture appears in the closing verses of Zephaniah."[1]

From 3:9 until the end of the book, we see hope. We see a description of the messianic era, the era of Jesus which will continue until the second coming. Zephaniah says God will **"purify the lips of the peoples."** I see a couple of ideas here: one is a reference to Isaiah 6 where God purifies the lips of Isaiah so that he can speak to the people on God's behalf. It could be that Zephaniah is talking here about God's purifying the lips of His people so that they can then speak on His behalf to the nations, fulfilling the Abrahamic promise of Genesis 12:3.

Another idea goes back to Genesis 11; this could be a promise of the reversal of the dispersion at Babel and the confusion of languages. At Babel, proud men united in their effort to build a tower to Heaven; here, Zephaniah speaks of the day when men will unite in the service to and worship of God – in real unity, not just a shadow of it. The men of Babel thought they could be the authors of their own security; God did not enter their equation. Here there is a promise of the Genesis process going into re-verse: we are brought back to Eden, into perfect provi-sion, rest, and security. The people will serve God **"shoulder to shoulder,"** which is also translated "in one accord." Literally, "with one shoulder" – what a picture of unity!

Judgment will purify. The remnant will call on God's name and worship and serve Him. Note that the word for serve also means worship; when we serve, that's an act of worship.

God's judgment is not the final word in Zephaniah's message; God's judgment is meant to be redemptive! God's character includes holiness, justice, righteousness, and an intolerance of sin; but remember that it also includes love, grace, mercy, and forgiveness.

In verses 11-13, we see that the Temple Mount, God's holy hill, will be free from haughtiness and pride, one of the major sins involved in an endeavor to live without God. And in verses 14-17, the people are told my favorite command in this book: **Rejoice!** Rejoice in the grace of God! The messianic era is described vividly. It will be a time of great joy when the Lord will be in the midst of His people. Palmer Robertson says of this: "God breaking out in singing! God joyful with delight! All because of you."[2]

Zephaniah says in 3:17:

"The Lord your God is with you, the Mighty Warrior who saves. He will take great delight in you; in His love He will no longer rebuke you, but will rejoice over you with singing."

I love this picture of God! How many people see God like this? Not enough I'm afraid. Can you see the powerful and amazing imagery that Zephaniah paints for us of a God who rejoices over us? That just astounds me every time I read it.

Verses 18-20 close the book, not with the people's joyful response to God's goodness (we saw that in 14-17), but with further blessings promised by God. There will be relief from oppression, separation, and suffering. The work of redemption as well as judgment belongs to God alone.

In chapter one, Zephaniah mentioned idolatry as the first problem among his people, but he quickly moved to the problem underlying it: the trust and worship of one's own opinions and desires. Our pride, arrogance, and trust in self and wealth are summed up in 3:5a – **"the unrighteous know no shame."**

But hear me - we don't have to live that way anymore!

That's the old way; there's a new way that was shown to us by Jesus. In Jesus, we have reason to sing Zephaniah's song of victory. If the Holy Spirit is living in us, then everything is different, and we need to live that way!

Leaders: **Are you living in judgment or rejoicing in grace?**

Without Jesus, we remain in judgment, facing a life without God and an eternity separated from Him. In Jesus, we find hope NOW – we find life NOW – we find what God is promising through the prophet Zephaniah. This is not talking about the afterlife – this is NOW – it's happening – it's on!

You and I get to choose how we're going to live this life – this one and only life that we have. **Are we going to live in judgment, trying to earn God's favor through what we do, or are we going to rejoice in the grace and freedom** that comes only through Jesus?

If we allow this to, it can change every aspect of our lives, from how we view ourselves to how we view others to the words we use and the thoughts we think.

Jesus offers life – real life – living in grace, not judgment. But like the people of Judah, we have to take him up on it.

PRINCIPLES FROM ZEPHANIAH:

- God is just, not fair.
- What you worship determines what you become.
- Prideful arrogance separates us from God; humility brings us closer to Him.
- You can't look down on others when you're facedown in the dust.
- Are you living in judgment or rejoicing in grace?

9 CONCLUSION

In this book, we've talked about principles for leaders from six of the twelve "Minor" Prophets. My hope is that you have learned the immense value of these (not so minor) books! I also hope you've learned some things about these men of God and their short prophetic books that you didn't know before. But more than that, I hope that you've seen in their words principles for your life and leadership. God never wastes anything; I've seen that to be true so many times in my life, and I believe that the words He gave to these prophets were for our benefit as well as theirs. We have to do the work of digging through their time and place in their historical and cultural context, but when we do that, I believe we can learn MUCH from these men and their lives.

My intent is to complete a second volume in the future that will deal with the other six Minor Prophets, but as I close this volume, let me thank you for taking the time to read it. My goal with this book was to create something useful and beneficial for those seeking to lead. Don't for a minute, though, think that this is an exhaustive study of principles from these prophets – far from it! If you will read them, spend time with their words, and grow in your understanding of their place in history and their culture, you will undoubtedly see even more. The rabbis used to say that Scripture is like a seventy-sided jewel; every time we look at it, we see a new perspective, something fresh and new. That has been my experience with these (not so) Minor Prophets, and I hope it will be yours as well.

ENDNOTES

Chapter 3

[1] R. T. Kendall. *Jonah: An Exposition – The Lessons of Jonah for the Church Today.* London: Authentic, 2006.

[2] Douglas Stuart, *Hosea-Jonah (Word Biblical Commentary).* Waco: Word Books, 1987.

[3] Phillip Cary. *Jonah (Brazos Theological Commentary on the Bible).* Grand Rapids: Brazos Press, 2008.

[4] Robert B. Chisolm, Jr. *Interpreting the Minor Prophets.* Grand Rapids: Academie Books, 1990.

Chapter 4

[1] Costen Harrell. *The Prophets of Israel.* Nashville: Cokesbury Press, 1933.

[2] Lloyd J. Ogilvie. *Hosea, Joel, Amos, Obadiah, Jonah (The Communicator's Commentary).* Dallas: Word Books, 1990.

[3] Simon Wiesenthal. *The Sunflower.* Schocken Books, 1976.

Chapter 5

[1] J. Alec Motyear. *The Minor Prophets: An Exegetical and Expository Commentary.* Grand Rapids: Baker Books, 1998.

[2] Ibid.

[3] Robert L. Alden. *Daniel and the Minor Prophets (The Expositor's Bible Commentary)*. Grand Rapids: Zondervan, 1985.

[4] Mark J. Boda. *Haggai, Zechariah (The NIV Application Commentary)*. Grand Rapids: Zondervan, 2004.

[5] Pieter A. Verhoef. *The Books of Haggai and Malachi (The New International Commentary on the Old Testament)*. Grand Rapids: William B. Eerdsmans Publishing Company, 1987.

[6] E. B. Pusey. *The Minor Prophets: A Commentary*. Grand Rapids: Baker Book House, 1956.

[7] James Wolfendale. *Commentary on the Books of the Minor Prophets (The Preacher's Complete Homiletic Commentary)*. Grand Rapids: Baker Book House, 1980.

[8] Alden, *Daniel and the Minor Prophets*.

[9] Mark J. Boda, *Haggai, Zechariah*.

Chapter 6

[1] Palmer Robertson. *The Books of Nahum, Habakkuk, and Zephaniah (The New International Commentary on the Old Testament)*. Grand Rapids: William B. Eerdsmans Publishing Company, 1990.

[2] John Ortberg. *Know Doubt*. Grand Rapids: Zondervan, 2008.

[3] Page Kelley. *Micah, Nahum, Habakkuk, Zephaniah, Haggai, Zechariah, Malachi (Layman's Bible Book Commentary).* Nashville: Broadman Press, 1984.

[4] Stephen R. Miller. *Nahum, Habakkuk, Zephaniah, Haggai, Zechariah, Malachi.* Nashville: Holman Reference, 2004.

[5] Page Kelly. *Micah, Nahum, Habakkuk, Zephaniah, Haggai, Zechariah, Malachi (Layman's Bible Book Commentary).*

Chapter 7

[1] Willem A, VanGemeren. Interpreting the Prophetic Word. Grand Rapids: Zondervan, 1990.

Chapter 8

[1] Palmer Robertson. *The Books of Nahum, Habakkuk, and Zephaniah (The New International Commentary on the Old Testament).*

[2] Ibid.

ABOUT THE AUTHOR

William Attaway serves as the senior pastor of
Southview Community Church in Herndon, Virginia,
a commuter suburb of Washington, D.C.
Originally from Birmingham, Alabama, he and his wife
Charlotte live in northern Virginia with their
two daughters.

Made in the USA
Charleston, SC
22 September 2014